CEO
FOR LIFE

CEO
FOR LIFE

Gain Full Control of Your Life and Your Business Forever

Robert Lee Barber

LEON SMITH
PUBLISHING

This book is dedicated to the women in my life who challenged me to be the best CEO for Life. It is also dedicated to my Creator.

To my mother, who passed unexpectedly in 2018: You gave me all the skills and fierceness to take on a demanding world. Even though you were a single mom, I watched you maneuver the personal and business world like a masterful conductor. I miss our talks every day. We will see each other again in all God's glory. Thank you, Mom.

To my family, Jalonne, Savannah, and Kennedy: You make me want to be better every day. There is no greater achievement for any CEO for Life than significance over success in those around you. You all are my greatest achievements as a CEO for Life. Being a dad and husband is so humbling. Thank you for trusting me. I hope I listened to you enough. All my love, girls.

To God: All is your glory, as we always talk about. "Send me." (Isaiah 6:8) You are a good, good Father.

CEO for Life Map

CHAPTER 9

CHAPTER 10

Acknowledgments

This will be a failure, as I know I will miss someone critical to the writing of this book and the journey leading to its inception. Here is a first swing at it. I appreciate you all.

Karl Moeller: my business partner for thirteen years and best friend. Thank you for always teaching me to pause, trust God, not take everything so seriously, and most of all take time to smell the roses. Oh, and closing solves everything.

Alex Jansen: for believing in me from the first time we met. You bet on this little auction company. You are a calculated risk-taker and visionary, and a wonderful husband and father. I'm proud to have been your partner and more importantly, your friend.

Ronn and Leah Filley and Larry and Anna Kelleher: for being lifelong friends. Thank you for accepting me as I am and always being there.

Keith Leon: my publisher, who took a chance on this guy with a crazy idea. From the first time we met, I knew God's hand was on the friendship.

Joel Marion: thank you for always pushing me to go bigger. To think bigger.

Marsha Friedman: a supernova shining light in an otherwise dark world. Thank you for believing in me.

Sandy Sembler and John Hall: two of the coolest people the universe has connected. You both inspire me daily. Thank you.

Michael Cross: thank you for being my first real client. You bet on me, allowed me into your inner circle, and invested in me as much as I did you.

The Utmost Boys Thursday Devo Men—you all know who you are: I couldn't do life without our Thursday time, all the conversations and coffees, and cocktails in between.

Jim Keener, CEO Sentient Energy: You had a profound impact on me, helping me to develop the confidence to be able to do anything I set my mind to. Thank you.

Sean Dwilet: my cousin, but really my brother and partner in crime. Somehow, with our wildly strong current of an upbringing, it is all working out the way it was supposed to. I love you man, as a brother.

Introduction

Your Thinking Has to Be Right

Just as in the dictionary, fear comes before reward.
~ Robert Barber, CHPC

If you feel like you are failing to be the best version of you, it is because the most difficult step is the first one. Where should you begin?

Starting is scary; it is actually terrifying. Nobody gives a shit about you or your messages—at least not yet. You have to believe that you and your message matter. If you believe this, you are headed in the right direction. Please take this to heart. Take courage; there is an answer. Today, you start moving toward the best version of yourself by reading this book.

The start comes with first understanding that you are the *CEO of your life*—for life. In 2006 and 2007, I was almost broke when I had this realization. I explain those details later, as I show in extreme, real-life terms how this paradigm saved me and can help you.

Have you ever felt like a superhero? Or wanted to be one?

Did you know the world is counting on you? On us? These are not egotistical statements. They are fact. The entire world is depending on us to be the best version of ourselves, to be *superheroes* in our own lives. Let's pivot from the comic book version of a superhero to the concept of being *CEO for Life*. It is easier for me to relate my life with the role of a CEO than a fictitious character with superpowers. CEOs run businesses, achieve goals, pour themselves into and invest in their teams, have accountability, make mistakes, get fired, face challenges, know how to celebrate wins and losses, and are real people walking among us. CEOs are not mythical creatures.

So why does CEO seem a logical place to start?

With my experience in executive level Human Resources, growing a company from two states to twenty-six states in just five years, I was exposed to the good and bad of leadership. This included Fortune-150-level executives from varying backgrounds, corporate experiences, military backgrounds, and entrepreneurial backgrounds. From this experience, I was able to design what I think is a solid job description for a CEO. With the *CEO for Life*, these requirements and this framework apply to life and work. I call them *life-place* and *workplace*.

Below is how a *CEO for Life* Job Posting would look:

Summary

We are seeking an experienced leader to oversee and set strategic direction for both the life-place and workplace. You are the one responsible for all company decisions as they relate to the strategic direction. You are responsible for creating a vision those you manage or interact with can engage for success. You must be a direct and decisive decision maker who can inspire those around you. You must have a mindset that can focus on the bigger picture, but also have a pulse on the small things that can lead to challenges. You must be able to focus on successful metrics for finances as well as metrics for people.

Willingness to learn or have experience in the areas of Vision casting, Strategic planning and short-term goal setting, Finances, Operations, Human Resources, Communication, Governance, Ethical Standards, and Continued personal growth.

Responsibilities

- Have an entrepreneurial mindset that can balance risk and reward—including the operational and organizational decisions.

- Have an experience base that includes communication, marketing, finances, Human Resources, and self-awareness.

- Have strong knowledge and track record of ethical governance.

- Execute the right thing all the time, regardless of the immediate challenges that may occur.

- Possess strong problem identification and problem-solving skills.

- Demonstrate strong speaking skills, in public and internally.

- Demonstrate a willingness to learn and understand market conditions that can impact both the life-place and workplace.

- Build internal and external relationships that are key to the company's success.

- Be willing to act.

- Maintain a level of transparency with all stakeholders.

- Execute investment strategies that will align with long-term financial goals over short-term gains.

- Oversee the rollout of all activities that impact the strategic vision and the short-term goals that will lead to the success of the company.

- Motivate all those around.

- Make tough decisions to allow only those who are contributing to the success of the company to remain in the organization.

- Develop the vision and strategic direction as well as thoroughly communicate it to all stakeholders.

- Attract the highest level of talent to all levels of the organization.

Now let me ask you a question: Do any of the roles, responsibilities, and expectations sound like what you do or should be doing every day in your own life?

Take a moment to answer the following:

- Does the buck stop with you on how well you do on any given day?

- Do you set directions and strategies for your life, your family's life, your work life, and your relationships?

- Do you decide whom to hire and fire in your life?

- Do you manage your budget?

- Do you need to make sure you are making the most revenue for the shareholders in your life?

- Do you meet your goals on some days and not on others?

- Is your growth equal to the investment you make in yourself?

- Do you experience competitors and obstacles?

We could go on and on matching the job description to life in general, in the workplace, or in your personal life. That job description could easily describe how you are to run your life.

In the following pages, I will make a case for you to live that life in the workplace and your personal life as well. The *CEO for Life* is aligned with not only the best version of you in the workplace, but also you as a *CEO for Life* of your life—the best version of you, for you, and for those in your life. If you are an individual contributor, manage a team, own your own business, or contribute to the family daily by managing a home, you will always remain the CEO for your life. You cannot quit this job.

Our world is becoming more focused on entrepreneurship, celebrating people who are multilevel marketing, multimillion-dollar masterminds, influencers, athletes, and those who have huge podcast followings, social likes, and the best Tik Tok videos. A person really can be a singular business and multimillion-dollar profit center. The obstacles that used to hold people back from achieving what they want have almost, but not completely, been eliminated due to the internet and a person's willingness to work.

People are talking about being a leader and being better by investing in oneself with courses, books, coaches, meditation, and a number of different techniques. But no one is connecting the tried-and-true concept of being a CEO of their life first and what that could mean if that title connected to their life. This connection is foundational. Napolean Hill knew this in 1926 when he published *The Laws of Success*. He knew CEOs—like Dale Carnegie, Henry Ford, Edwin Barnes, and others—had something we needed to learn. He interviewed all of them extensively to find the secret sauce. I argue there was no difference in their work life and personal life. They never took off the CEO hat. So, take that concept and run your life inside and outside the workplace, in relationships, and in your home as the CEO.

Let's take a minute to unpack a bit more the title of CEO because it is important to embody the mindset. First, you must accept the role; you must want the job. You were hired the day you were born.

I have had many people ask me why I call the book *CEO for Life* and not *CEO of Life*. The word *of* implies you have the ability to allow someone else to be the CEO of your life. I don't believe that to be true. You are the only person in control of yourself and your outcomes. You could give others control, but that would still be your decision. You are your own CEO, and that role is for your lifetime. The role does not go away; you cannot quit this job. You cannot give it away. You cannot be fired from it. Think of it as being *CEO for Life* of your life.

You cannot delegate the responsibilities; you deserve all the accolades as well as the difficulty of failed outcomes for the decisions you make. These truths represent a mind shift. This book is not about behavior or feelings. It is about a new paradigm. How you think will drive how you feel, and how you feel will drive how you think, therefore impacting how you behave and the subsequent outcomes in life. It's time to start thinking like a CEO in all aspects of your life.

People with that job title think this way. I bet Jeff Bezos, Elon Musk, Bill Gates, and Warren Buffet treat every aspect of their lives as if they were the CEO. I first had this realization when I quit my six-figure executive position for a Fortune 150 company to pursue owning my own real estate company. In the end, it was my decision to make this change, and if it all went bad for my family and me, that result was on me—no one else. And, it was on me to make the next chapter in our lives work. Yes, we worked as a team, but in the end, I shouldered much of the weight to make it work.

Let's blow this up a little—like that scene in *Iron Man 2* when Tony Stark expands the 3D hologram of a new element into an exploded view—and look at a bigger picture of this new paradigm. Think about it for a moment. If you are living life like the *CEO for Life*, you impact everything around you by the decisions you make and your behavior. Multiply that result by billions of other people acting as their own CEO in the world, also taking responsibility for themselves.

Would there be a major change in the world?

I dream about each person grabbing hold of this paradigm and the consequent impacts. That collective rippling process could change and impact the world in ways no superhero or comic could imagine.

In the next chapters, we explore what it is like to be the *CEO for Life* and what it takes to be that CEO. It is a learned process that you need to practice every day. This book is an introduction to the concept of being your own CEO. It is about developing that mindset.

CEO for Life. You may have never even considered that as your Life Title. You may wear other labels, like Mom, Wife, Dad, Brother, Sister, Girlfriend, Employee, Rehabilitating Addict, Depressed, or Alcoholic. But whatever other labels you may wear, you are in control and steer the ship of life. You are the CEO of your life; you are your own *CEO for Life*!

At the end of each section of this book, there are opportunities for self-reflection and discovery activities. If you do not put them into practice, words lie dead on a page. It's up to you to bring these words to life. In the coming pages, you are asked to reflect, think, write, and answer some hard questions about you as your own CEO. The purpose is to move out of your comfort zone into one of *CEO for Life*.

Take the simple words from the pages and bring them to practice in your life. Actionable change should be your goal. I have this hope in my heart for you. Please commit to trying all the chapter activities and assignments that you are asked in this book. This is how you invest in you.

This paradigm has been in my heart for a long time because it is real for me. It is in my DNA. But I never knew I was acting like a *CEO for Life* until the moment I left my corporate position. Living out those thought processes and behaviors was how I was raised. I was raised to think in terms of no labels or defined descriptions.

For me, there was no other way to live life than following the belief that *I was the one responsible for my outcomes*. It was up to me to make things happen in my life. I am sitting here right now writing these words as I have just sold my interest as a partner in a company that sold over $917 million in real estate alone last year. This was my third real estate startup. The company is only seven years old. However, using my CEO skills, I knew it was time for a pivot to a new business venture and time for a change for my family.

Why was I selling my interest in a super-successful company? The answer is simple. My vision, mission, and goals had changed, and I knew I needed to follow what I saw as the future for my family and me. This was CEO decision-making in real life.

I was told I was crazy, off my rocker; my friends looked at me funny. I was walking away from ongoing success to pick up my family and move from Tampa, Florida, to Chattanooga, Tennessee, to start an entirely new business in an area where I knew no one.

However, *I am the CEO for Life*. I had a vision, my family was onboard, and I was going to execute my vision. CEOs must make tough decisions, even when they are contrary to comfort and normal thinking. What I want to impress upon you is that I live out what I am writing, and I am encouraging you to do the same. This book is not theory for me. I encourage all my coaching clients to think in these terms, and I have witnessed their success as a result.

Now, before you get tied up in knots about that last statement, the decision to make serious life changes is never done in a vacuum. I discuss decisions with people I look up to, just as a CEO does with their board. I had my family's full endorsement, just as if they were major shareholders. I developed a plan and executed that plan—and I am still executing that plan. Those are CEO attributes.

The reason for sharing this story is to reinforce the fact that *I walk the talk*. I want you to know I live out what I am asking of you.

Discovery Activity:
Two Ideas I Want to Pursue and Two Regrets

Let's take a few minutes and put some of what we talked about into perspective. On the next empty pages, write down two ideas you would love to pursue in your life, as well as two regrets. Then write down your age.

Two Ideas I Want to Pursue and Two Regrets

Two Ideas I Want to Pursue and Two Regrets

Ideas and Regrets

With those two ideas and two regrets in mind, consider this: *Fortune* magazine said in 2018 that, on average, individuals may work until age 69 and die at 78.7.[1]

I will use myself as an example. I am forty-eight at this time.

Years left to work: 69 − 48 = 21

Years till dust: 78.7 − 48 = 30.7

If I have 21 years left to work—and only 30.7 to live, I am not going to wait to do the things I know I want to do. I have already lived long enough to know how fast the years go.

How many years do you have left based on this exercise?

Now look back at what you wrote down as your two ideas and two regrets.

This is not meant to scare anyone into action; these are just facts. From the moment you were born, you were already working up your own corporate ladder of life to be the CEO you were meant to be—the CEO for God, yourself, family, friends, relationships, your work, the world.

This rant was to put the issue of *time* into your mind as you go through the remainder of this book. *Time is something*

---

1 fortune.com/2018/02/09/us-life-expectancy-dropped-again

you cannot get back. That is why it is serious for you get the concept of *CEO for Life.*

Here's another way to look at it: In the CEO equation, the average work year for a U.S. worker is 2,080 hrs. There are 8,760 hours in a year. What are you doing with the difference between those two, 6,689 hours?

We talk about self-investment later in this book. But let's talk obstacles for a minute.

Do you think you have obstacles that will keep you from pursuing life changes?

You may be thinking:

- *Well, Rob, I didn't have the best upbringing.*

- *You just don't know my situation, Rob.*

- *I am recovering from some serious stuff in my life.*

- *I am just trying to make ends meet.*

Respect. *Major* respect. I get it.

Here's some background about me for context. My mom became pregnant with me at age seventeen. She made a major *CEO for Life* choice by keeping me. Let that sink in. That statement was not judgmental; it was real. There was an incredibly tough choice to be made, and she made it. Her dream was to be a New York fashion designer. She gave up that dream to have me. She went to nursing school instead to generate revenue to support us. *CEO Boss*. Much respect to my mom.

At age eighteen, she was married and shortly after, divorced. Another CEO choice. We then moved from our little mobile home in South Jersey to Florida with everything we owned packed into a Volkswagen bug, with me in a bassinet on the floorboard. Another CEO choice.

My mother made major choices in her life that drove outcomes. She had vision, mission, drive, and support, but still had sleepless nights and tough choices, and she always told me she wouldn't have done it any other way.

My mom died this past year at age sixty-five, unexpectedly. It crushed me. A friend of hers with whom she'd remained friends since high school told me that she said her proudest achievement in life was me.

Through all the hard times, my mom never complained. She taught me to do the same. She overcame any obstacles and taught me to do the same. She grew three successful businesses and lived a life worth celebrating. She was a person worth emulating, for me and for my two daughters.

My mother had vision, mission, goals, and action in her DNA. She fired people from her life when they didn't align, stayed the course through curves and turns, and always stayed true to doing the right thing because, as the saying goes: *The right thing to do is always the right thing to do.*

Those lessons helped me be the *CEO for Life* of my life, but we never labeled it that. It took owning my own business to realize that I was the label and paradigm, *CEO for Life*, even though I was living out the principles in this book. I got my degree in electrical engineering because I knew that job would make good money. I had the big job in human resources and labor relations—with only one person between me and the CEO—in a multi-billion-dollar business. I was overseeing three thousand employees in twenty-six states at age thirty-five. My *CEO for Life* upbringing made all the difference.

We live in a time when anyone can rent a jet and a Rolls Royce, stand in front of them to take a picture and claim they can help you find your purpose and reach your goals. I have learned that *the real givers don't give advice.* Instead, they lay out a path for you to find your own CEO path. They ask you great questions, suggest activities, and present challenges that push you to be *uncomfortable*, because that's where the magic happens. In that uncomfortable zone. And most importantly, these people will tell you that *it doesn't happen overnight*. It may take twenty years.

And *here is where I will let you in on a little secret.* Remember that 78.7 years? *The journey is what it is all about.*

It's about the joy in the valley, when it's all crashing, as well as the joy on the mountaintop. Because now, you are able to pass along the benefits and wisdom of your journey. This is how you impact the world as the *CEO for Life*.

Before we jump into the meat and potatoes of how to unleash the *CEO for Life* in you, let's answer a question:

Why should you listen to anything I have to say?

I really want you to know I have lived my life this way, and you can as well. I have always had in my DNA the building blocks of a CEO. For me, that means I take responsibility for what I want in life. I forge the path to my goals and then act to bring them into being. This includes the relationships in my life. At every stage, I have had a vision for what I wanted my life to be, built a mission toward that vision, set goals, and then executed them. It was natural for me. I never saw the obstacles even though at times they were considerable. I always saw past them and always moved forward.

As mentioned, I was born to a young mother of seventeen years. We grew up together, with only each other. We had plenty of hard times, but that never kept my mom and me from going after what we wanted from life.

High School and College Years

In late elementary school, if I wanted something, I found a way. For example, I sold cinnamon toothpicks in school to make extra money. My mom always stopped at the convenience store in the mornings before dropping me at the bus stop. I would buy fireballs and apple bubble gum and candy to sell in school, in addition to the toothpicks. The spring training facility for the Texas Rangers was near my house, and I would go there and shag foul balls in the parking lot to sell them. I carried them around in a big tube sock. I also bought and sold baseball cards signed by the players.

I joined ROTC in high school because I wanted to be in the military. The closest school participating in that program required me to take two public buses to and from school. Instead of playing sports, I forged my birth certificate to get my first real job in the mall at a fast-food joint. I waited tables all through high school at an assisted-living facility. That really opened my eyes. It became clear to me how I wanted my life to end up. Did I want my life to be regret-filled? Or full of joy? Certainly, full of joy.

I never had a plan to go to college, but through fortuitous circumstances, I ended up at a local college in Florida. I had no idea what I wanted to do, but I knew engineers made good money, so I pursued a degree in electrical engineering. I also knew I needed a group of people around me whom I could count on and who could count on me. I pledged a fraternity, and to this very day, at forty-eight years old, I am still friends with all my brothers. I can call them and they can call me at a moment's notice, and we are there for one another. My experience with the military also taught me about the benefits of having a tribe, a squad, or whatever you want to label it.

Professional

Soon after college, I realized I hated being an engineer, but I loved people. I found a way to get into human resources (HR). I worked thirteen years in HR. I wanted to go after an MBA during that time, but I was traveling a lot, so I went after my MBA online. Again, I found a way. In that time, I pioneered bringing HR into new parts of the business. When I left my position, I was an executive in a Fortune 150 company with HR responsibility for more than three thousand employees across twenty-six states. Professionally, I have recruited, hired, fired, trained, developed, and managed employees across a variety of professional experiences and geographies. I've negotiated some of the most difficult situations anyone could imagine.

Entrepreneur

Those experiences reignited and fueled the interest in entrepreneurship I've had since my early childhood. While working in corporate, I would hear executives use the cliché: *You wouldn't make that decision if it were your money or your company.*

I always thought: *I want to know that feeling. I want to experience having my own company.*

I wanted the make-or-break decisions on me. I no longer wanted to hide behind a corporation.

I came home from a trip one day and told my wife I wanted to start my own business. She, as always, said, "Let's do it." She is amazing. My wife and I have been married for twenty-four years and have two beautiful daughters. By the way, being the *CEO for Life* also applies to dating and intimate relationships, although we won't talk a lot about these issues in this book. It could be a topic for a book in the future.

In 2006, I went to school at night to get my real estate license. I quit my corporate job and moved my family to a location within our target market area. In 2007, the real estate market imploded and I didn't make any money for a year. I found myself living in the red for the first time since leaving college. Mind you, I also had a family at this time and some debt.

But that pressure pushed me to find a great partner and start a business that was needed. We founded the most successful real estate auction company in West Central Florida, and we did it during the downturn. When the market turned, we invested as partners in a retail real estate company with a relationship we had built in the downturn. That company had sales of $917 million in 2018—within just seven years of opening doors.

With that under my belt, I felt comfort creeping in. I happen to think comfort is a disease. When I get too comfortable and I'm not being pushed to grow, I feel compelled to make a change. Therefore, in 2019, I sold my interest in the real estate company, and gained my certification as a high performance coach from the High Performance Institute. There are only two hundred of us Certified High Performance Coaches (CHPCs) certified per year worldwide. The certification must be renewed every two years. It is based on studies conducted with 174,000 participants as the foundation of the Certified High Performance model.[2]

This new endeavor functioned to refresh and reinforce what I had already learned through experience. At the time, I launched the ROYI (Return On Your Investment) Academy, my new coaching firm, and again moved my family to another part of the country to experience a new lifestyle and capitalize on a new market that I felt needed my company on the ground. In addition, it was out of our comfort zone, and I was looking for a new challenge.

In the humblest way, I am the first to say I surely don't have all the answers, but I do know that you are *CEO for Life* in your life. Everything comes back to you. I can help you take on this role in your own life. These are principles I have lived, proven, studied, and been invited to teach.

Whether you are just starting off, down and out, on the mountaintop, or wanting to take your life and business to the next level, I can help you.

---

2 www.highperformanceinstitute.com/blog/measurement

In summary, the combination of my life experience, proven results, and certifications in High Performance coaching provide the basis for you to seriously consider what I am writing. I want you to be the best version of you. My hope is that this book acts as a pseudo-coaching mechanism for you.

My belief is that coaching is *a living mirror*. When you hire a coach, you are really getting a questioning reflection. A good coach will help you look at yourself and recognize what needs improvement as well as where you are excelling.

As you read this book, I ask that you treat yourself like a business while you work through each section and set of activities. This is serious business. We are talking about you being the best version of you. If you can't get behind that, then just hang it all up now and accept a mediocre life that will be nothing more than a whimper. I make no apologies for the harsh talk. You picked up this book for a reason, so get serious about becoming your CEO, or give this book to someone else.

I encourage people to become a basic member of the ROYI Academy. You can find details at ROYIACADEMY.com. The more CEOs we have running things at home, work, church, other groups, and even on the streets, the more I believe we will see a positive change in our communities.

So, let's do a little work getting you down the road. The activity and discovery sections of this book will be categorized in three main sections: *Start, Discover,* and *Lead. Start* is all about getting your mind right and prepared. Just as it is for athletes, the race is won way before you step on the field or court. The *Discover* activities are designed to remove the obstacles you have put in your own way to keep you from being the *CEO for Life*. Believe it or not, it's *you* keeping you from what you want in this life. *Lead* activities are designed to help put the concepts covered in the book around being the *CEO for Life* into practice.

My situation was full of challenges and they continue today. Perhaps yours are too. I do not minimize the difficulties of your story; in fact, my hope is the difficulties you have faced will help to drive you.

Eight Ways to Think Like a *CEO for Life*

Everyone has the capacity to be the CEO in their own life story. Here are eight steps to help you to start thinking like a *CEO for Life*.

1. Define

First, define the difference between workplace and life-place. One is how you will achieve success at work and the other, outside of work.

2. Take Ownership of Your Decisions

Fully embrace the idea that you will receive all the accolades and all the blame. This level of ownership is a heavy weight in life, but why would you want to give your success or failure away?

If you want to be a CEO, you must be prepared to take full ownership of all decisions, both good and bad. When you do this, you will eventually see there really are no bad ones, just those that you learn from. A CEO is able to get things done, even if resources and assistance are not available. A CEO doesn't care if they have to do it all. I have emptied the trash cans at night after having closed the biggest deals that day. As the CEO of your life, you will begin to relish and take ownership of the decisions in front of you. You will actually look forward to the challenging decisions as they will be the most rewarding. You will even relish making a decision to remove a bad habit, because you are doing it for you and those around you who depend on you. So many of us have been conditioned to play a victim role. We have been conditioned to look to others to save us from our mistakes the way we did as a child. Listen, I am a parent with two incredible daughters. You have to let them fall from time to time to learn. Life does not care who your mom and dad are. It is you that matters. At some point, begin to relish your own messes. That will make you a better *CEO for Life*.

3. Planning, Planning, Planning

Planning is key. A CEO needs a plan. Doing something amazing requires thought, and CEOs have big, bold plans. Throw caution and sensibility to the wind, and make a plan worthy of a CEO. I recommend your plan should have a timetable no longer than ninety days. Even if you want to take on something that may take a year, squeeze it into ninety days. You will be surprised by how much gets done. A *Balanced Scorecard* or *Objectives and Key Results* (OKR) approach is an excellent way to plan.

If you are not familiar with the Balanced Scorecard system, it is a methodology developed in the 1990s to help organizations map vision, mission, themes, and strategies and eventually align an entire organization. It is an excellent process. I am certified as a Balanced Scorecard Professional, and I have executed this process numerous times for corporate clients and my own business.

OKRs are a tighter scope of objectives with shorter time frames. Many technology companies, like Google, use them over a Balance Scorecard Approach.

I happen to be certified in both, because they both provide excellent results.

4. A Plan Is Useless Without Action

Thinking and planning are essential, but nothing happens until action is taken. A plan is useless unless action is taken. You can build a boat and sit on shore for the rest of your life. Only those who are willing to get in the boat and navigate to new shores will reap the rewards. Doing something is better doing nothing.

Do you overplan? Too often, people *plan to paralysis.* Sometimes clients plan, plan, and plan to the point that the plan itself becomes an obstacle to progress, making them unable to move forward. This excessive planning results in a kind of paralysis.

I am often asked, "How do I know I have the right plan?"

The answer is, "There is no right plan."

Make a plan and then execute it. People are not failing from planning but in *failing to start.* Remember, you are the CEO. Your 80 percent is probably better than most people's 100 percent. Get started now.

Elon Musk says, "Take your ten-year plan and try to execute it in six months. Yes, you will fail but you will get a lot of stuff done."

5. Reject Excuses

I picked this concept up from my upbringing and more recently, from military school. In officer training, there were never excuses, only improvements. Excuses are for non-CEOs. CEOs ignore excuses and make things happen. Obstacles are meant to be overcome.

6. Thinking Is Critical

Thinking is critical, but the word *critical* is in there because it is also time-sensitive. Speed is better than an overthought plan. You will quickly find out the sooner you act, the sooner you can get the data you need. The sooner you act, the sooner you can make the adjustments required to get you where you want to go as a CEO for your life.

7. Rooftop or Lobby?

Being in the lobby is comfortable. There are nice chairs, people to serve you, and often a bar or restaurant. But the lobby is for those who just want to be comfortable.

Why do people get stuck and fail to make progress?

In many cases, it is because they simply have gotten comfortable or complacent. When you get satisfied, the creep of laziness comes calling. Be scared of comfort.

If you think to yourself: *$50K/year is good enough. It's a decent salary, and I can comfortably pay my bills*, you're not ever likely to earn $50K/year. I had a roommate in military school who was fond of the adage: "Shoot for the moon. Even if you miss, you'll land among the stars."

CEOs set higher standards. I call them *rooftops*. I have a few principles that I stick by. One is that I think comfort is a disease. Comfort scares me. When I am on the rooftop, it is a bit scary, but I feel alive. If I'm not stretching, I know I am not going to achieve what I need to.

8. Never Allow Your Values to Slip

This is the greatest temptation. There will be days that you feel so beat up that the easier path seems so tempting. Stay true to your values and filter every decision by them. This must be a rule.

CEOs respect these things about themselves and refuse to sacrifice. I call it *the CEO compass*. I have a compass tattooed on my right arm. It reminds me of my true north. I will not deviate intentionally; if I find I am deviating unintentionally, I need to course correct. I also need to ask: *Why was I beginning to deviate?*

Is your current way of thinking getting you where you want to go, or is it holding you back? Take these next blank pages to write down the answers to these questions:

Start Activity: Are You Thinking Like a CEO?

What is your current way of thinking about your life?

What do you _want_ your thinking to be?

Who or what in your life is limiting your thinking?

Now that you have answered these questions, the next sections are going to begin to put the pieces in place to move from your current way of thinking to a new way of thinking as a *CEO for Life* of your life.

Are You Thinking Like a CEO?

Chapter 1

Your First Day as *CEO for Life*

What is the worst thing about yourself that you like?
~ Amit Abraham

This quote always makes me laugh because of its honesty. We all have things we hate about ourselves that we like. For example, I absolutely suck at organization, but I really don't care; I embrace it. I have others help me with organizational tasks.

This chapter is about self-assessment. Do not skip it. Don't wait until the end of this book to start your self-assessment. The biggest failure for anyone reading this book will be the failure to start.

Say to yourself: *No longer is "fake it till I make it" good enough*. Your first day starts and ends just like everyone else's. It's okay to make a bunch of mistakes along the way. It just makes your journey more memorable.

Here's where your practice should start. It's okay if you don't have all the answers today. It's okay if you're not perfect. We all have the same challenges. When to start is your decision, yours only. You cannot push that on anyone else. You must own it. You already know you are the *CEO for* Your *Life* from the first chapter. So, let's get to work.

For giggles, let's think of this moment as Monday morning. The morning has arrived. It's six o'clock and your alarm is going off. You hit snooze four times. Somehow, you muster the energy to get out of bed and contemplate the challenges of the day. Suddenly, you grasp your chest and immediately know you need to call 911.

The *New York Times* in 2006—thirteen years ago, mind you—before many of us got involved in social media—found that the risk of a heart attack was about 20 percent greater on Mondays for adult men, and 15 percent greater for adult women.[3] Most researchers have blamed the stress of returning to work for the increased risk, but I happen to think it is because people don't have the right mindset. They feel controlled by life rather than feeling in control of it. The only authority I have to speak on this is I have lived my life both ways. I have dealt with anxiety since my early twenties. You can ask my wife of almost twenty-five years. Some mornings, I don't want to get up and go. But then I lean on

---

3 nytimes.com/2006/03/14/health/the-claim-heart-attacks-are-more-common-on-mondays.html

the fact that I am the CEO. I know that moving forward is a whole lot better than sitting still in my anxiety. So, I get up and begin my day. I know you can do it too. Please, just start.

I don't claim to have data or an alphabet soup of credentials to prove my thesis that Monday mornings suck for almost all of us. But it is certain that Monday morning will arrive. So will the other 364 mornings in a year. You can bet on four things right now. The first two are death and taxes, to which I have added: 3. *The sun will come up*, and 4. *The sun will go down*.

What am I getting at?

Time is short. Every CEO understands this and knows that *now* is the time to be the best CEO they can be. You must start now to form habits to control your life, to become confident that a solution will always present itself, and to be the best you can be.

CEOs don't live their life by a workweek. They don't work for Fridays. They don't dread Mondays. Every day is an opportunity to excel. Grow. Dominate.

Let's talk about habits next. They will be a foundation for your next steps.

Habits and Discipline

Let's unpack the concept of *habits* for a moment, with reference to their importance in the *CEO for Life* mindset.

Most every CEO focuses on two things: *results* and *results*. Why is that? Because this is the way we are incented. As in any situation, the behavior that is reinforced and measured is the one that will win and continue. CEOs are forced to deliver certain results quarterly and are then compensated on how well they achieved those results. At the same time, they are paid the big bucks to take the company to the next horizon and are expected to foresee any obstacles and challenges before they come. It is the same for your life and mine. We must look at the future, but we cannot live there.

The secret to mastering yourself, your daily world, and your success as CEO is *habit* and *discipline*. On this, your first day as the *CEO for Life*, we will be talking about your daily habits and how they are likely to impact your effectiveness as CEO. What are your daily habits? Can they be improved?

First, here is a quick definition of the word *habit* from Webster's Dictionary: *a settled or regular tendency or practice, especially one that is hard to give up*. Think about your habits. Take a look at any part of your life and consider how your habits have influenced it. Good habits are supportive. Negative habits are destructive. With the right habits, you can have the ultimate power over yourself and your life.

Do your habits control you, or do you control them?

The first thing any good Balanced Scorecard professional will do for an organization is *assess*. Let's do that.

Discover Activity: Self Reflection – Good and Bad Habits

Answer these questions to gain a better perspective:

1. What is my written vision for my life?

2. What is my mission in life?

3. What are my goals?

4. What habits are helping me reach my goals?

5. What are my negative habits? How are these habits harming me?

6. What is the most important habit for me to create?

7. Which of my negative habits is most necessary to give up? How would this help me?

8. What are the mistakes I've made this week or month, or in the last ninety days? What can I learn from them?

9. What would help me remain focused every day?

10. In what areas of my life do I feel out of control? What habits can I create or eliminate to restore equilibrium?

Self Reflection – Good and Bad Habits

Self Reflection – Good and Bad Habits

Strategies for Eliminating Bad Habits

- Deal with one challenge at a time. As they say, *eat the elephant one bite at a time*. Habits take time to change. Prioritize them.

- Be a scientist or detective. Be curious and adopt the perspective of doing some real digging and investigation. However, be careful not to spend too much time here. Overanalyzing can become a loop and rabbit hole that will stall your progress. Try different strategies to see what works for you to increase good habits and limit the bad ones. Use reminders on your phone to reinforce good habits. I love using alarms on my phone to remind me of my time-blocking, when to focus, when to meditate, and when to say *enough*.

- Tell your friends and family what you are trying to accomplish. Accountability is always helpful. And do not just tell them—ask them to invest their support in you.

- Write down your thoughts and record your progress. Journal. Each day, ask yourself what it would mean if you continued to indulge in your bad habit. Visualize the likely outcomes and write them down. You are 42 percent more likely to achieve your goals if you write them down.[4] It makes sense that this would correlate to habits as well. My daughter is excellent at this. She has a unique strategy. She journals the day and then throws it away. When I asked her why, she said, "This day is over. And I am on to the next." Mind you, she is fifteen.

- Give yourself permission to fail. Many of my clients are stunned when they hear me say this. No one else will give you permission, and if they do, it will come with judgment or advice. I'll tell you again: *Give yourself permission to fail*. You are not *perfect*; you are *progress*. Focus on controlling the outcomes you have control over.

Now the big question: What is really keeping you from starting the habits you want and stopping the habits you should?

Could it be *you?* Most likely, yes.

Habits for a *CEO for Life*

Now let's take this up a notch. Let's talk about *CEO for Life* level-up habits. From here, we can begin developing vision, mission, and goals. I want you to think of this as if you were an athlete tackling a marathon for the first time. There are

---

4 inc.com/peter-economy/this-is-way-you-need-to-write-down-your-goals-for-faster-success.html

certain habits that need to be reinforced, added, or cut out in order to build the plan to cross the finish line.

There are four critical areas to focus on to help you create the habits you will need to continue the journey of *CEO for Life*. They are:

1. Stop trying to be average: Be *you.*

2. Cultivate a servant mindset.

3. Invest time, energy, and whatever it takes in yourself.

4. Set boundaries and minimize distractions.

We talk next about each critical area.

Stop Trying to Be the Average: Be *You*

Think about the other CEOs you have surrounded yourself with. Are you their *average?* What does that mean?

Being an engineer, I often fall back on that training when I try to make sense of issues. For example, here are the three laws of motion in physics:

- Newton's First law of Motion: An object will remain at rest or in a uniform state of motion unless that state is changed by an external force.

- Newton's Second Law of Motion: Force is equal to the change in momentum (mass times velocity) over time.

- Newton's Third Law of Motion: For every action in nature there is an equal and opposite reaction.[5]

There is the *Human Law of Averages*, meaning that you are a direct average of the three people you spend the most time with. I want you to write down the names of these three people. I bet that you dress alike, watch the same shows, enjoy the same sports, finish each other sentences, have the same political views, date someone similar, and so on. Hence, the Human Law of Averages.

This is a detriment to you being the best *CEO for Life*. Stop trying to be the average of the company you keep. *Be you*. You were created for a purpose as an individual with your own ideas, thoughts, and decisions.

Remember when we talked about lifespan? Do you think your time in this world is an accident? Even if you don't believe in a worldview outside yourself, you have to admit you have one time around in this life. There is a beginning and an end. Each one of the 108 billion people who has been born on this planet has had their own story.[6] You are your own CEO with your own brand and unique story. Be conscious of who you surround yourself with, but don't become their average.

---

5 "Newton's Three Laws of Motion." Stanford University. ccrma. stanford.edu/~jos/pasp/Newton_s_Three_Laws_Motion.html
6 prb.org/howmanypeoplehaveeverlivedonearth/

Cultivate a Servant Mindset

CEOs pour into others first—they serve others. A common trait between all successful leaders over the long term is that they put others before themselves. They act in a sacrificial way. They know that by giving first to others, they will get more out of those people and achieve the common goal. I first understood this concept while in Military School at Valley Forge Military College.

I was in an accelerated officer program that required us to be a part of the National Guard as well. And like all National Guard and Reservists, you spend time at drill weekends, keeping your skills sharp. I was part of a Recon unit.

One weekend, we were to spend the entire drill in the field. Meanwhile, the temperature had dropped into the twenties. And of course, yours truly had mistakenly left his harsh weather gear in the barracks. After getting a nice yelling-at and some carefully designed calisthenics, my Sergeant Major gave me his harsh weather gear. He was sacrificing his comfort and well-being to take care of his soldiers. This sacrificial attitude runs all through the military. Another example is that officers do not eat before their soldiers. If anyone is to go hungry, it will be the leaders.

This always stuck with me and is a common thread in how I lead in the life-place and workplace. If you have not heard of the idea of *servant leadership*, get to know it. Think about what that idea means to you.

Do you look around and find ways to serve others? This is the sign of a superior CEO. Create a servant mindset.

> *No one has ever become poor by giving.*
>
> ~ Anne Frank
> *Diary of Anne Frank*

I really saw this truth during my days in HR serving employees across twenty-six states. Even though I had a title and was on some organizational chart higher up the chain, my team and I always looked at our role as serving the employees. That service included everyone from executives to plant management to the people on shift. We went into every situation asking: *How can we serve?*

Unions would come in from time to time and attempt to organize the employees. They would promise to represent the employees' best interests. But the employees already had a team of people who cared about them and their needs, a team that put their interests first, listened, and worked night and day to serve them. There was never a need to have an outside entity serving them.

This also goes for home relationships. Your family and relationships will get what they need from you, or they will find it elsewhere. If you take an inventory of the people you served during one day, I will show you how successful you were that day. However, if you string enough days together in which it is *all about you*, you will run into serious challenges as *CEO for Life*.

Invest in Yourself

CEOs invest in themselves. Investing in yourself will lead to habits that we will talk about in the next section. Investing in yourself is a critical component of your first day as a CEO and every day after. A CEO on their first day will bring their habits with them, so let's focus on your habits for a moment.

What are your habits? How can you create habits that invest in you and your vision?

I wrote down my vision and placed it where I can see it every day. Reading my vision statement daily encourages me to persevere. When I look at my goals, I ask myself: *What I can do today to come one step closer to accomplishing them?*

Constantly reflecting on my purpose helps me keep my actions focused on the big picture. Whether or not I achieve my calling in life rests on my steadfast determination to act responsibly every single day. Faithfully performing my mundane daily tasks creates great success for me. Accomplishment is something I must work for daily. Even after I have achieved a level of success, I continue to work hard to maintain it and improve on it.

Your habits can either promote your success as the *CEO for Life* or diminish your chances. Each day you can make a choice to excel in the small things—habits—in order to position yourself on the path of success. You must resolve to form habits that are beneficial to your overall goals.

I watch other people, and when I see someone who is successful at something I want to master, I observe and select some of their positive habits to imitate. YouTube is one of the greatest tools ever to come along for CEOs. If I want to learn to do yoga, bake a cake, change the oil in a car, fly a drone, base jump, train for a triathlon, all I need to do is type it in the YouTube search bar. If I have a bad habit, I can search for answers and lessons from people who have beaten the same bad habit.

There are no longer any excuses for ignorance when it comes to habits. You can learn to create and break habits and the only person stopping you is you. For example, I am determined to cut out of my life those things that waste time and hold me back. No matter how long I have performed a behavior, the strength to retrain my brain can be found within me.

Read the sentence below:

Today, I choose to take an inventory of my habits and only keep those that benefit me.

Repeat this sentence to yourself. If you need to, do it every morning. Even set an alarm on your phone. Through the power of self-control, you will eradicate useless practices from your life and use your time and energy for more positive behaviors.

Set Boundaries and Minimize Distraction

On day one, focus is critical. It is also critical on days two through forever. I was given a book called *Boundaries: When to Say YES, When to Say NO, to Take Control of Your Life,* by Henry Cloud and John Townsend (Zondervan, 1992). It was game changer for me. I had always thought I had set good boundaries, but that was not the case.

Our ability to focus has been reduced dramatically; we've never had more distractions to deal with. As disheartening as it sounds, much of our environment was engineered to be as distracting as possible. We live in the age of attracting as many eyeballs as possible to get attention. Hey, I will admit I have an Xbox, I love social media, and I binge-watch Netflix and Amazon Prime for escapism. It is my responsibility to keep these distractions under control. That is one reason I love screen time notifications each week. I challenge myself to know my boundaries and recognize when my balance is off.

Our brains can quickly become addicted to these distractions; some of them may cause a dopamine effect. This means that scrolling, Liking, tapping, fast-forwarding through shows, and binge-watching may create a feeling of accomplishment that is addictive.

Our ability to cultivate beneficial habits will suffer because of distractions. Learning how to focus is a vital skill if you want to be productive and successful. After studying and working on building my own habits, I have some recommendations for you.

Here are eight strategies that can help you to overcome the distractions in your life:

1. The One Thing Instead of Everything

Avoid fooling yourself. Multitasking is a sham. I have a timer on my phone and a set of time-blocks that keep me focused on one thing at a time. I don't even answer phone calls during those times. All the critical people in my life know my schedule. You'll get more done and feel more relaxed if you focus on a single task at a time. *Time-blocking* is a masterful skill that will change your life. Run your life; don't let life run you.

2. Eat the Frog Early

There is a great book by Brian Tracy entitled *Eat That Frog! 21 Great Ways to Stop Procrastinating and Get More Done in Less Time* (2017). In the book, Tracy tells us our ability to focus deeply is greatest in the morning and decreases throughout the day. Make sure the items you focus on first are the ones that you are avoiding or seem most painful. Get them out of the way. A few people also do well late at night, if their day isn't too demanding, but it is usually advisable to schedule your more demanding mental tasks earlier in the day. Save the simpler items for later, when your focus is weaker—or allow some rewards for later in the day, like a hobby, time with family, meditation, or exercise.

3. Practice, Practice, Practice

You can't be good at something you don't practice. It's more difficult than you think to focus deeply. Try setting a timer for fifteen minutes. Keep your attention entirely on performing a single task. Notice how stray thoughts constantly interfere. Notice how strong the urge to check your email, text messages, and visit social media becomes. Over time, you'll be able to focus for longer periods before you need a break. Think of it this way: Your brain needs a workout as much as your body does.

4. Love Being Bored

When you're focused and working, you can also be bored. I daresay monotony can set in. Most of us choose to distract ourselves when we're bored or when we want to be doing something else—something we like better. The better you can handle boredom, the easier it is to avoid engaging in those distractions. When you have the urge to distract yourself, force yourself to wait just fifteen minutes longer. After a few days of this, try thirty minutes. Keep building on this. Remember, you are providing a workout for your brain.

5. Purposely Remove Distractions

Create a space for you that will keep you focused on the tasks at hand. If you have deadlines coming up, put your phone away. Change your voicemail to let people know you will call back later in the day. Go on the offense with your time.

6. Redirect Distractions Using Signage

Signage is by far the most effective tool for creating boundaries and killing distractions. Put a Post-it note on your door letting people know when you will be available. Create a table card that lets people know you are busy and place it near you with what you are doing. People will respect it. Create voicemails and do-not-disturb times on your phone and email with autoresponders, letting people know when they will hear back from you. People will always assume you have time for what they need. You need to directly tell them when you will be available to them. This will allow you to respect each other's time and enable you to be at your most focused for that person when you do schedule a meeting.

7. Reward Yourself With Distractions

You can time-block to address distractions. I am not saying you need to live a silent life in your room to be a *CEO for Life*. Intentionality is what I want for you. No successful CEO lacks intentionality, even with their escapism and distractions. You don't have to avoid your favorite distractions 100 percent of the time. Simply schedule time for those activities after your work has been completed for the day. Put a reasonable limit on how long you'll spend on your distractions.

8. Nighty-Night

A regular sleep schedule is vital, and you can easily look up the science that supports this idea. Friends give me a hard time because I am strict about my sleep schedule, but I know how my body and mind react when the sleep schedule is disrupted.

Life is a never-ending series of distractions, but the most successful people are able to focus in spite of distractions. It takes practice to focus intently in the face of other things vying for your attention. Incorporate these tips into your daily schedule and you'll see your ability to focus grow. You are the only one stopping you from developing habits that will take you where you want to go. That goes for bad habits too; they will take you somewhere as well. Where you go is up to you.

Don't give up yet! Yes, you may have heard these tips for creating success before, but ask yourself why have you not gone after it? Why aren't you implementing these concepts? Why aren't you living your *CEO for Life?*

Executing a vision is the most difficult part of the process. It is where most people falter. The rest of this book is dedicated to guiding you step-by-step through the execution of your vision. Together, we chart your path toward *CEO for Life* with vision, mission, values, and goals.

Chapter 2

Dream Generational

*Make your vision so clear
that your fears become irrelevant.*

~ Anonymous

Generational Thinking

The phrase *dream big* is so overused. *Dream generational* is a far better term. Dreaming big is about you, while dreaming generationally is a real vision for a future forever changed because you cared enough. A CEO always puts others first. The *dream generational* thesis encourages us to be H2H, meaning *human-to-human*. The foundation of this idea is the servant mindset.

Here's the real stretch: *Are you willing to dream for all those around you first?* This is the kind of thinking that drives results and creativity, simply because it reflects more than just you.

Generational thinking causes you to:

- Make different choices

- Make bigger sacrifices
- Love more than what you are doing now
- Love those you are doing it with
- Focus on what you mean to the people around you

Finding your meaning in others will drive results. It may seem contradictory, but it is the foundation of a successful vision.

Creating a Vision for Your Life

When you read the word *vision*, what do you think? How does the word relate to your life?

For a long time, I thought vision was a fluffy, pie-in-the-sky idea or dream. It was something like a plush toy—squishy and fuzzy, something to keep me safe at night when I went to bed. It is that plush, fuzzy, teddy-bear perception that needs to be dispelled.

As soon as you read the words *creating a vision for your life*, your brain probably glazed over. Why is that? Because most people think of *vision* as that pie in the sky, as I did. Early in my career as an engineer, I can't tell you how many times my bosses would talk about company vision in in corporate meetings. I would mentally roll my eyes.

Internally, I would be thinking: *Company vision? Who knows the vision for their company? Who even has a vision for their life? Isn't the term just for consultants to make money?*

In 2007, I had an idea of what I wanted to do as a commercial realtor, but no vision set in stone. When faced with the Great Recession of 2007–2009, I had to get serious. I knew I was not going to go backward—to my old job—although I could have done that.

To get serious, I refined my guardrails and my vision. My new vision was to become a Certified Commercial Investment Member (CCIM), which is effectively a master's degree in commercial real estate that must be backed by millions of dollars in transactions. I was killing two birds with one stone. My vision would necessitate me completing transactions, which would, in turn, generate income. My vision became my fuel to survive and then thrive.

Vision must come *first*. However, most people either discount the concept of a vision, or don't know what it is. Now, I am not discrediting them or questioning the validity of their opinions. What I care about more is getting results for you. Vision is the catalyst for your success as the *CEO for Life* of your life.

Organizations may spend millions of dollars developing their vision statements, but take no time to ask teams what their vision is. Does the team vision match the company vision? Shouldn't that matter? All organizations need to care about each human being and their vision for their life. The team and their vision will determine the direction in which you are headed.

I can tell you that during my thirteen years in corporate roles, I never once invested in the vision. I heard it; I knew it—but I did not internalize it. I saw it posted on walls and on websites, but as I worked for different bosses, I often saw that vision did not translate to the individual behaviors of those who must execute the vision.

The most common reasons for this situation are:

1. The vision is not clearly lived out from top to bottom in an organization.

2. The compensation structure is not tied well to the actions that will accomplish the vision.

Do not misunderstand me. I am not saying in any way that they were bad bosses. I am grateful to all of them for different reasons. However, the system was almost contradictory to having or supporting a vision. During each performance review, I was asked about my next assignment, but we never really talked about what I wanted for my life. I can tell you the answer to that question changed quite a bit over those thirteen years. If those conversations had happened—who knows?—I might still be there.

Take a poll. Ask the most successful people you know if they have a vision for their life or have ever gone through the process of exploring their vision. Then ask the same thing of those who seem stuck in life. I bet most don't have the slightest idea about their goals, let alone a vision for their life.

Stop and ask the questions: *Do you think having a vision will allow you to create a future for you to work toward? If you are the CEO, shouldn't you have a vision?*

The Relationship Between Vision, Mission, and Goals

I want to explore the idea of vision again, but maybe from a different angle, because it is vital that you internalize the idea of vision as a *CEO for Life*. I'll use an example that I sometimes use with clients. It incorporates the concepts of vision, mission, and goals.

Imagine that my *vision* is that I want to travel from New York to San Francisco. My *mission* involves what I need to get me from NY to San Francisco—a car, gas money, GPS, time off work, and so on. My *goals* are the fractional parts that get me from mile to mile. For example, I need to get in the car, I need to fill the car up with gas, I need to point the car in the right direction, I need to have hotel arrangements in Chicago, and so on.

The overarching theme here is a crystallization of the vision, moving from the big idea to the individual steps to get you there. But imagine if you didn't know you wanted to go to San Francisco. You would be on an aimless journey. The vision is the compass that drives all other actions in your life.

The vision is your bigger picture. It is the black box through which you will filter all major life decisions. As Simon Sinek puts it, your vision is your *why*. His book, *Start with Why:*

How Great Leaders Inspire Everyone to Take Action (2009) is an excellent resource that I highly recommend. He also has delivered great Ted Talks and made videos on the subject.

What Matters to You?

Your vision—your *why*—is a deep internal compass that has long-range directional impact. There is no set rule that says that your vision cannot change. In fact, I bet it will. Vision is something to revisit in three-to-five-year increments or after major life changes.

For example:

- When I was eighteen, my vision was that I was going to be a fighter pilot.

- When I was twenty-five, my vision was to be an amazing engineer and husband.

- When I was thirty-five, my vision was to own my own business and dominate real estate.

- When I was forty-eight, I wanted to apply the past twenty-six years of entrepreneurial and life experience and pour it into others with my own coaching and consulting company. My vision was *Five in Five*: five thousand people impacted in five years.

Discovery Activity: Self-Reflection:
What Matters Most to Me?

Your vision will be created from what matters most to you at this time of life. A good self-reflection exercise is to make a list of five things that matter most to you.

What matters most to you?

1.

2.

3.

4.

5.

Here is my list:

1. Faith

2. Family well-being

3. Pouring my life into others (legacy)

4. Fighting regrets

5. Being uncomfortable as much as possible

The minimum should be five items on your list, but feel free to add more. Within those categories, write down your dream or vision for your life. This will be your working *Vision Statement*.

Here is my Vision Statement as of writing *CEO for Life*:

> *I will focus on a life filled with activity, intentionally carving specific time for my family, as well as my faith, while building my new brand that will ultimately have an impact on as many people as possible. Five in Five: I want to impact five thousand people in five years through the Return On Your Investment (ROYI) Academy, my new coaching company, using my life experiences to help them be the best version of themselves.*

As you see, my vision at age forty-eight focuses on number 3 on my list—*pouring my life into others*—but does not neglect the others.

Don't worry about grammar. Don't worry about it being perfect. Just put it into words that resonate with you—words that you are willing to hold yourself accountable for.

When I wake up, I think: *Five in Five.* As you break down my current vision statement and unpack it, you will see woven in the words the five categories on my list, tied together with the wrappings of another factor: *time.*

I care a lot about time as a part of my vision. I am willing to be patient, but I am not going to be paralyzed. I will not sit back and not take action. As I sit and write this, I am currently thirteen days away from moving my family to Chattanooga,

Tennessee, to pursue this vision. I sold my shares of our real estate company to make that happen, a company that sold over $917 million in real estate last year. I care so much about my vision for my life that I am not going to let anything stand in the way of its pursuit. Regret is too costly.

There is a striking video in which Gary Vaynerchuk, a successful business person and global media CEO, is asked to sum up motivation in just three words. "You will die," he says, meaning you get one life.[7] One time around. So make it the best.

My first coaching client is a successful leader and a major get-it-done person. He leads a large team in multiple locations. On our first coaching call, we went through the process of discovery.

He discussed what he felt was working and not working in his life, both at home and at work. We spent about thirty minutes of our session focused just on this topic. I use this initial conversation as the basis for the future. It helps us figure out where we want to spend our time and what to focus on. What the session boiled down to was that he was struggling to make some decisions about next steps for him at work and life in general. These were next-chapter-type decisions.

---

7 "The Most Motivational Statement Ever In 3 Words." youtu.be/0wdUDD6HaC0

I asked the question, "Do you and your family have a vision statement?"

He said, "No. What do you mean?"

I explained that we are our own CEOs, no different from an organization with a CEO. As CEO, if you don't have a vision, how will you know where you want to go? Now, in fact, most all of us know where we want to go, but we don't focus enough to put it on paper in a concise statement. This vision statement should be one that is agreed upon by you and your family, although it can certainly change over time. Think of your family as the board of directors. They can fire you; they can guide you.

Support Your Vision With Your Habits, Discipline, and Mindset

Let's circle back for a minute and talk habits again. Everything we talked about in the first two chapters is foundational to becoming the best version of you as *CEO for Life*. Habits, discipline, and mindset support your vision. I have a clear vision written down in a place where I can see it every day. Cultivating the habit of reading my vision statement daily encourages me to persevere. After I look at my goals, I ask myself what I can do today to come one step closer to accomplishing them. Constantly reflecting on my purpose helps me keep my actions focused on the big picture. Whether I achieve my calling in life rests on my steadfast determination to act responsibly every single day.

Faithfully performing my mundane daily tasks creates great success for me. Massive change is, after all, the sum of many small incremental moves. I was once told that you could turn the world on its side if you had a long enough lever. You will have to ponder that one and picture it. It turned out that was based on this quote:

> *Give me a lever long enough and a fulcrum*
> *on which to place it, and I shall move the world.*
> ~ attributed to Archimedes

Accomplishment is something I must work for daily. We all do. Even after I have achieved a level of success, I continue to work hard to maintain it and improve on it. I remember my wife sending me a meme with the quote below:

> *My habits can either promote my vision or hinder it.*
> *Each day, I make the choice to excel in the small things*
> *in order to position myself on the path of greatness.*

I resolve to form habits that are beneficial to my overall goals. When I see someone who is successful at something I want to master, I observe their life and imitate some of their positive habits. I am determined to cut out of my life any practice that wastes time and holds me back. No matter how long I have performed a behavior, the strength to retrain my brain is found within me. Today, I choose to take inventory of my habits and only keep those that benefit me. Through the power of self-control, I eradicate useless practices from my life and use my time and energy for more positive behaviors.

Discover Activity: Self-Reflection –
Habits to Support My Vision

---

1. What is my vision?

2. Does it scare me?

3. What practices do I need to stop because they hinder my progress?

4. Which habits should I purposely form to accomplish my vision?

Self-Reflection – Habits to Support My Vision

Self-Reflection – Habits to Support My Vision

Creating and expressing our visions may come in different forms. We are different people. Some are visual, some auditory, some like to write, and some like to create with their hands. It can be daunting to develop a vision. Creating and displaying a *vision board*—a visual representation of your goals and dreams—can help. It may seem cliché, but it can be a wonderful tool to remind yourself about your goals each day.

One of the most challenging parts of achieving goals is consistently following through at a high level. It's easy to become distracted, beat yourself up, or even forget about why you started. I change my background and lock screen on my phone and laptop often to keep them fresh and motivating.

Vision casting is a solution for all these challenges. It's a process for attaching concrete goals, definitions, and timelines to your vision. Regular use of vision casting keeps your goals fresh in your mind. Using vision casting also associates positive feelings with the achievement of your goals.

Once you have set forth the vision, write it down. Share it with as many people in your sphere as possible. Out of every one hundred people reading this book, only one or two have a written vision statement for their life that includes a combination of personal and professional vision.

Once you have written your vision down, you can use it at any time. Keep it with you so you can refer to it whenever you want. You can summarize it in a few words if that works for you. My current vision statement is written on a green Post-it note in my wallet. It says: *Five in Five. I will help move the needle for five thousand people in the next five years.*

Creating a Vision Statement

How do you create a written vision statement that works? Here is a stepwise process that can help you.

1. Establish Goals

First, you must decide on your goals. This is often the most challenging part. For best results, narrow your focus to just a few goals, but make them big. Perhaps your goals are related to fitness, acquiring material items, or having a new experience. Right now, a big goal for me is to skydive. Last year, I was able to hang glide and it was amazing. This year, I will tandem jump.

Your goals are up to you. What excites you? What stretches and scares you?

2. Associate Your Goals With Imagery

A picture is worth a thousand words. Visualize the milestones or the micro-wins that will lead you toward the future you'd like to achieve. We touched briefly on vision boards. Create yours using pictures to help you clarify your vision. Search on Google Images for keywords of topics that excite you. There are plenty of sources for images: photographs, magazines, the internet, and more. Find pictures that best represent the goals you wish to achieve. Put them in a folder on your computer or phone. If you're striving for a new car, find the exact model and color. A Porsche was always my dream. I read every article on every new model and would often stop by the local dealership. When you look at the photo, you should get the same feeling you get when you think about the goal. If you have the pictures at your fingertips, you can recreate that feeling to fight off distractions or obstacles.

3. Establish Key Words for Your Vision

If you just add an S to word, you create a mighty SWORD. Words can be powerful tools for crafting your vision. When defining words for your vision, make them simple and to the point so that they immediately conjure what you are after as *CEO for Life*. A suitable word might be *Porsche* or *Honolulu*. Next, choose words that tell how you'll feel when the goal is achieved: *excited, grateful, proud*. Finally, select words that express the qualities you will need to achieve these goals: committed, powerful, or maybe optimistic.

4. Put the Words and Images Together

Gather these words and images together to come up with your written vision statement. A vision statement should not be wordy, but it should be lofty. It should help you remember where you are going, and why. Remember, your vision can be thought of as providing you with guardrails that will keep you on the path you have selected.

The creation of a vision statement is easy if you just follow the steps. You might even enjoy the process. It does not have to be a grandiose Gettysburg Address. It is simply a guiding light that will shine on your path, much like your car headlights.

How to Use Your Vision Statement

Like anything in life, just creating it is not enough. Using your written vision statement is just as important as creating it:

- Do not hide your vision. Your vision should always be right in front of you and others. You should be able to see it morning through night. If you're comfortable doing so, you could mount it on the bathroom mirror. I like to keep mine on my phone and in my wallet. Every time I reach for a credit card, it is there to remind me. Having your vision handy will keep you on track.

- Spend a few minutes each morning voicing and exercising your vision. Is it still your vision? Affirmations work. They align your neural self. This exercise can set the tone for the rest of your day. A good friend of mine taught me to take the first hour of my day and align myself with what I want that

Chapter 2

Dream Generational

*Make your vision so clear
that your fears become irrelevant.*

~ Anonymous

Generational Thinking

The phrase *dream big* is so overused. *Dream generational* is a far better term. Dreaming big is about you, while dreaming generationally is a real vision for a future forever changed because you cared enough. A CEO always puts others first. The *dream generational* thesis encourages us to be H2H, meaning *human-to-human*. The foundation of this idea is the servant mindset.

Here's the real stretch: *Are you willing to dream for all those around you first?* This is the kind of thinking that drives results and creativity, simply because it reflects more than just you.

Generational thinking causes you to:

- Make different choices

- Make bigger sacrifices
- Love more than what you are doing now
- Love those you are doing it with
- Focus on what you mean to the people around you

Finding your meaning in others will drive results. It may seem contradictory, but it is the foundation of a successful vision.

Creating a Vision for Your Life

When you read the word *vision*, what do you think? How does the word relate to your life?

For a long time, I thought vision was a fluffy, pie-in-the-sky idea or dream. It was something like a plush toy—squishy and fuzzy, something to keep me safe at night when I went to bed. It is that plush, fuzzy, teddy-bear perception that needs to be dispelled.

As soon as you read the words *creating a vision for your life*, your brain probably glazed over. Why is that? Because most people think of *vision* as that pie in the sky, as I did. Early in my career as an engineer, I can't tell you how many times my bosses would talk about company vision in in corporate meetings. I would mentally roll my eyes.

Internally, I would be thinking: *Company vision? Who knows the vision for their company? Who even has a vision for their life? Isn't the term just for consultants to make money?*

I have learned that the reason almost everyone has this view of the vision concept is because almost no one *executes* their vision. The words are just put on a board or poster in a hallway. It's like a diet you try or a New Year's resolution you fail to keep. It all sounds good, but you never stick with it or never believe it from the beginning.

The successful CEOs believe in their vision. They breathe it, sweat for it, and kick the ass of anyone who gets in the way of it. Let me put it another way. A vision is a map that helps you become the best version of you. You are a *CEO for Life*, but more than that, you are a mini-organization that requires a vision, because that vision will keep you from giving up or giving in. Your vision will help you motivate yourself, but it will also inspire and motivate others.

My vision is based on this idea: *A better world through better people.*

I believe I can impact five thousand lives in the next five years in my capacity as a coach at the ROYI Academy. I breathe in that vision with every breath, in every meeting, every encounter, every phone call or meeting I take. I live that vision in every chance encounter in the grocery store, meeting the guy across from me at the gas pump, greeting the young woman at the checkout counter, and so on. My vision invades my every thought, bone, blood cell, and heartbeat.

Guardrails

One good pictorial representation of a vision is the *guardrail*. Picture a set of guardrails along the road in front of you that are guiding your path. If you don't have guardrails as *CEO for Life*, you can easily go off the road, crash, and burn. Guardrails guide you along the outer direction of the road and give you enough room to swerve, speed up, slow down, and pass when you need to. The guardrails we give ourselves create the vision of where we are going. The guardrails allow your thoughts and actions to move forward in a specific direction.

Your vision trains your thought-life—what you feed your brain, which, in turn, feeds your heart, and therefore will guide your behaviors. As the old adage goes, *garbage in, garbage out*. Your behaviors form from your thoughts. From this vision, you form your mission, values, and goals. You create an organizational chart for your life—with results being measured—shareholders, and people hired and fired. When we fail to think in these terms and the structure falls away, issues may arise that allow uncertainty and chaos to enter the equation. Without guardrails, the next thing you know you are in a ditch.

> *The future belongs to those who believe*
> *in the beauty of their dreams.*
> ~ attributed to Eleanor Roosevelt

day, considering how it will take me a step closer to my vision. Reminding yourself of the importance of your goals each morning will point your brain in the right direction.

- CEOs have morning rituals. You need yours. Start today. Breathing, meditating, taking a walk, getting sun on your face—whatever it is that creates a higher state of focus. You'll see opportunities to help make your dreams come true. It's then your job to seize those opportunities. Look at each word. Take your time and visualize having those things in your life.

- Repeat your vision before bed. Your brain is highly active while you sleep. For most people, the brain spends all night churning away, trying to find solutions to your requests, planning for tomorrow's issues or challenges that may or may not arise. You have a high probability of waking up to the thought you last went to bed with. Why not make that thought your *CEO for Life* vision statement?

- Give your brain the information it needs to know it is all worth it. Allow it to rest in that calm water. Look at your vision and imagine possessing it. Experience how that feels. Part of your brain will spend all night trying to make your vision a reality. I even listen to videos and audio books while I sleep to help my subconscious keep a level of focus on what I want to accomplish.

It's not magic, though it sure may seem that way, especially as positive results begin to show. Keep your goals fresh in your mind by using your vision daily. Give it a few months and see for yourself how well it works.

Your Environment Matters

A CEO has to decide the best place for their headquarters. Setting matters. You have to take into account all the variables needed to accomplish the vision. As *CEO for Life*, you must decide whether you're living in the right place.

Does your current home location meet your employment, personal, and financial needs? Is it possible to achieve your goals there?

If not, consider your options. Are you willing to move away? If so, include on your goal list everything you must do to get ready to move. This is a critical one for me because it comes back to the thought of comfort. I really do believe that comfort is a disease that can kill you—meaning that it can severely limit your life.

I have moved around a bit in my life and each time that discomfort bloomed growth and success in fulfilling my vision for my life. I've lived in New Jersey, Tampa, Ft. Lauderdale, Philadelphia, Orlando, West Palm Beach, San Francisco,

Dallas, Juno Beach, St. Petersburg, and now, Chattanooga, Tennessee. Each move was a calculated decision to take advantage of the discomfort that comes with this kind of change. You must be willing to move to be the best version of you. There is an entire world waiting for you to connect. Don't stay in one place too long.

When I took hold of my new vision of *Five in Five*, I knew I needed to find the right environment, an environment that was ripe, to get me to my vision. Hence, in July of 2019, I picked up my family and we moved from our Tampa Bay home of thirteen years. My environment and all the variables that go with it had to match my vision.

Lead Activity: Vision Casting

The goal is to express your vision on paper and be able to articulate it to others. Use the vision board process defined above, consider what actions will bring the vision from your unconscious, and then guide you to your mission.

Layer on questions like:

1. What is the purpose of your life?

2. What do you want it to look like at ages eighteen, twenty-five, thirty-five, forty-five, fifty-five, sixty-five? Stick to ten-year increments.

3. Whom do you want in your life at those increments?

4. In which areas of life do you feel you could have the biggest impact?

5. What do you want people to say about you at your funeral?

Vision Casting

Vision Casting

Chapter 3

Make Your Life a Mission

Make your life a mission—not an intermission.
~ Arnold H. Glasgow, American Psychologist

How Do You Get Where You Want to Go?

With vision on its way and guardrails in place, it's time now to start thinking about how to accomplish your vision as *CEO for Life.*

The headlights are on, but how do you get where you want to go?

The first thing you must understand is the importance of deciding where your time goes. When it comes to accomplishing a mission, you need to realize time is everything. A CEO values time as if it is their most precious commodity. They guard it like Fort Knox.

I have a colorful picture of a watch behind me in my office that my clients face directly. They have to look at it, physically and subliminally, when they come to my office. Time is a topic I mention constantly in my meetings. If you were a fly on the wall during one of my days, you might hear words like: *time is precious, time is everything, you cannot get time back, why did you spend time on this, why didn't you spend time on that*, and so on. You decide where your time goes. Keep time in mind as you begin to build out the mission to accomplish your vision.

Vision Statements and Mission Statements

You have probably heard the terms *vision statement* and *mission statement*, but you may not know the difference between them. One of the main reasons people do not sit down and put pen to paper to define their vision and mission statements is that they have never been taught how. Another reason is that people think it is a waste of time. They don't understand that these statements are *the foundation of their life timepiece*. When you construct these statements, what you are building are gears and springs and hands—the parts that will drive the process of how time is used in their life as their own CEO.

The difference between vision and mission is simple:

- Vision is where you want to go.

- Mission is how you get there.

It's that simple. Say, for example, that my *vision* is to own a five-star restaurant. Well then, today, my *mission* is to attend culinary school for the next two years to get me the skills I need.

Writing a Mission Statement

In almost every major organization, these three simple questions are used to come up with the mission that supports their vision.

1. What is it we do every day?

2. Whom do we serve with what we do?

3. How do we serve them?

The best way to start any personal mission statement is with the words, "I will provide . . . " Then you include what it is you will do every day, for whom, and how you will do it.

Here is my personal vision statement, which you've already seen in the last section:

> *I will focus on a life filled with activity, intentionally carving specific time for my family, as well as my faith, while building my new brand that will ultimately have an impact on as many people as possible, using my life experiences to help them be the best version of themselves. Five in Five: I want to impact five thousand people in five years through the ROYI Academy, my new coaching company, using my life experiences to help them be the best version of themselves.*

In contrast, here is my personal mission statement:

Every day, I will provide as many opportunities as I can with the ROYI Academy to improve my health, to focus on my family, and to connect with and pour into people and their organizations.

This supports my *Five in Five*. You can see here that my mission statement is more focused on what needs to get done to reach my vision statement. I have narrowed it down to my health, my family, and wrapped it in the ROYI Academy to support and push my vision forward.

Visions and Missions Are Not Rigid

I formed a vision statement and mission statement mentally in 2005. I'd had this vision: *Create a commercial real estate company that that will generate $100 million in sales in less than five years.*

I established my goals and got my license as part of my mission, quit my Fortune 150 executive job, and jumped right in to building this vision. Well, the market decided otherwise and crapped all over my vision. Or so I thought. I did not give up in 2006 and 2007. Instead, I rallied to my vision. By the end of 2007, the vision changed a little, in that I found an amazing business partner and we created the most successful auction company in the West Central Florida area during the downturn. We auctioned real estate for just about every major servicer, bank, developer, and brokerage you could name. We did over 850 auctions and well surpassed the $100 million in sales. The vision had some caveats, but the guardrails were in place. I want you to see that visions are not rigid. A vision has a center line, but also has the flexibility of the guardrails.

Another way to think about mission is in terms of the military. For example, a war is made of a series of missions or battles. A vision is made up of missions. From a personal standpoint, another example to guide you is parenting. I have two daughters, ages fifteen and twenty. I realize parenting is a lifetime pursuit with a long horizon. I have a vision for my children's lives, but if I parented every day with only that long-term vision in mind, without breaking it up into short-term missions, we'd never get there.

Right now, knowing my fifteen-year-old, I can predict that in the long term, she is probably going to be a business owner on her own. But at the same time, she is entering high school, so we focus on that mission while interjecting opportunities to build something of her own. My twenty-year-old is probably going to be a teacher or counselor. However, right now, we are focused on getting her the training she needs today to move the ball to that vision for her life. Without the missions—that enable my children to acquire the skills they need—they would never be able to grow into the vision for their lives.

Have you ever asked anyone if they have a mission or vision for their life?

I was at my doctor's office once, having a great conversation with one of the staff. We were talking about my move to Chattanooga. They were telling me about what they want for their life.

I asked, "Well, what are you doing to get where you want to go? Do you and your family have a vision and mission statement for your life?"

They responded, "What is vision and mission?"

It is not their fault they don't know. These things are only taught in business classes. This is a life lesson. You are the *CEO for Life* of your life. This is your business course. This is where you start. Do not underestimate these first two steps of vision and mission. You will be shocked at the conversations that result in your own mind or with your partner and or family.

This is critical to understand: Vision can be singular— meaning that, in theory, it can be achieved in the long term on your own. Mission is likely to be more of a team concept, requiring connection, relationships, and support.

Now, why point this out? My experience is that missions are better achieved by working together, working like a SEAL team. I love studying SEALs and their process, how they operate as teams. They embrace the beauty of the team structure. They know techniques and skills as individuals and they know the vision of the SEALs. At the same time, each and every mission they tackle is based on the team approach. The makeup of teams is based on skills, roles, needs assessment, and the end goal in mind.

Personal Mission Statements

> *A mission statement is not something you write overnight . . . But fundamentally, your mission statement becomes your constitution, the solid expression of your vision and values. It becomes the criterion by which you measure everything else in your life.*
> ~ Stephen Covey, in *The Seven Habits of Highly Successful People* (2015)

Whether your mission is lofty or more down-in-the-weeds depends entirely on you. Here is a sample:

> *I will wake up every day with the mind to first serve others, then serve myself. This attitude will help me achieve success as a coach, a father, and a friend, leading to a life that will have balance between working, traveling, growing, enjoying life, and leaving a legacy.*

Your version could be much more specific. Notice that there is legacy involved in this example, capturing the impression you want people to summon when they think about you.

Lead Activity: Create a Mission Statement and
Give Your Life Direction and Purpose:

Vision is where you want to be tomorrow; mission is what you are doing today to get there. Note that writing a mission statement will take time. Mission statements are usually the most rewritten, and they tend to be longer than vision statements as they have more categories and detail.

What will you have to do to make your vision a reality?

Start with your vision statement. Actually write it down, and make sure you have settled on the content.

1. Now look at the categories that support your vision. Categories can include those things that are either life-place or workplace. For example, if my vision is to travel from New York to San Francisco, then categories would include *car, navigation, fuel, what to pack.*

2. Consider your strengths.

3. Look online for a few examples from people you admire. Several CEOs and other famous people have posted their mission statements for the world to see. Check out a few and see if anything appeals to you.

4. Reflect on how a mission statement may have helped you.

5. Try steps in your mission statement. If categories are not working, try thinking of your mission in steps. Steps make it a bit easier to visualize the mission that supports the vision. For the earlier example, in which I want to travel coast to coast, I ask myself what are the steps necessary to get me on the road and then to my destination.

6. Keep in mind that goal-setting is next. The steps or categories of the mission must be broken down into specific goals.

7. Don't be your own obstacle when it comes to taking action; this can be the most challenging part. Many of us like imagining and planning, but balk when it's time to actually take action. Avoid allowing this obstacle to halt your progress. Use this *80/20* rule: If you feel 80 percent good enough about what you have, then go with it. That 80 percent is going to put you in the top 20 percent, meaning that, most likely, 80 percent of your competition have not even considered this process. That puts you in the top 20 percent in your market or industry. In other words, 80 percent is good enough. It will put you in the top 20 percent of any industry because speed matters more than perfection, except in rocket ships.

A mission statement forces you to evaluate your interests, values, and priorities. Also consider your death and your legacy.

Take the time to complete this important exercise. You're bound to learn things about yourself you never knew and to re-energize your passion for living. If you want the best possible chance of living an amazing life, a mission statement is crucial.

Tip: Keep it brief and memorable. It should inspire you. If it does not, how well will you be able to communicate it? How do you think the people you are trying to lead will feel when they read it? If you are not jumping up and down, then start over.

Construct your personal mission statement below in the space provided.

Create a Mission Statement and
Give Your Life Direction and Purpose:

Create a Mission Statement and Give Your Life Direction and Purpose:

Chapter 4

Setting and Knocking Down Goals

Our goals can only be reached through a vehicle of a plan, in which we must fervently believe, and upon which we must vigorously act.
There is no other route to success.

~ attributed to Pablo Picasso

Using Goals to Chart Your Voyage

This is honestly my favorite part of the *CEO for Life* job: setting and knocking down goals. Why? Because goals provide instant gratification. At least they are for me. As I am a bit of a type A person, I like to see results and quickly. I tend to make goals short-term so I can see progress. Notice, I did not say the goals I set are easy or they do not stretch me. I just like to set goals that are shorter term to achieve. Goals keep me motivated, even if I do not achieve them. I wake up in the morning with daily goals in mind to set the stage. It is in my DNA. Some may set goals, and if they do not achieve their goals, they become discouraged. That is not the case for me.

I try to set short-term goals that are easy to measure. With my background in engineering, I love numbers and measuring. *Measurable goals* is such a business textbook term, but making goals that are trackable and measurable does matter.

I am sure most people have heard of SMART goals, developed by George T. Doran.

A SMART goal is:

- Specific
- Measurable
- Attainable
- Realistic
- Trackable

Let's go a little deeper.

Consider the process of setting goals as an adventure you are about to embark on. So far, we have developed the vision and set the milestones or missions that will get us there. Now we need to identify the goals that will support that vision. Goals function as the *chart* on this voyage. They will enable the voyage to be broken down into measureable increments that tell us if we are making progress.

You will actually come alive much more once you've set your goals. Every little goal reached will boost your self-confidence and your enjoyment of life. You'll banish boredom because there's always something to do and a pot of gold to look forward to at the end of your rainbow.

Dare to Set Big Goals

How big is your pot of gold—a cup, a dump truck, or the size of the Grand Canyon? Please let me impress upon you that your goals need to match your vision. Dare to set big goals.

A perfect example is when the United States made the bold decision to move forward with a crewed mission to the moon. The United States' Apollo space program was born, resulting in the Apollo 11 landing on the moon. This was the first crewed mission to land on the Moon. On September 12, 1962, President Kennedy announced to the world that the U.S. was going to the moon. That was the vision. To dream that big meant a huge mission and big goals. Especially when you consider the computing power of the Apollo 11 spacecraft was one hundred thousand times less than the iPhone 11. Think about that. Most calculators in kids' backpacks have more computing power than the Apollo 11.[8] Dare to dream big goals so that big vision can be accomplished.

---

8 Kendall, Graham. "Apollo 11 Anniversay: Could an iPhone fly me to the moon?" *Independent*. 09 July 2019. independent.co.uk/news/science/apollo-11-moon-landing-mobile-phones-smartphone-iphone-a8988351.html

Goal Setting

Everything in life has a process, and goal setting is no different. Let's unpack the process. Here are the most important factors to consider when you are setting goals:

- You must be motivated by your goals.

- Your goals should be realistic.

- Your goals should be easily measureable.

- Goals may need to change along the way.

- Plan a daily routine that moves you toward your goals.

- Understand that you will encounter obstacles.

- Get support.

We'll talk about each of these topics below.

Motivation

Are you motivated by your goals?

Goals must be yours. When asked whether someone should pursue their dream, build a business they want, quit school, and flip shoes, and so on, marketing and media-thought leader Gary Vaynerchuk asks the question, "Who are you doing this for?"

If you have the vision, mission, goals, and values in front of you, it better be for you. If you aren't pursuing this dream for yourself, it will never come to be.

Now don't get me wrong. Are there going to be goals that you won't like pursuing? Yes. Just like that last set of squats. Do you really want to do them? Are you more than likely going to puke? Maybe. But it needs to be done.

Let's go back to Brian Tracy's book, *Eat That Frog!*, in which the author calls doing the things you don't want to do *eating your frog*, and recommends they be done as your first tasks of the day.

This expression is derived from something that Mark Twain is reputed to have said: "If the first thing you do in the morning is eat a live frog, you can go through the rest of the day knowing the worst is behind you."

Your frog is your worst task or goal, and you should do it first thing in the morning.

I was recently told about a book, written by another professional coach, called *Hope Is Not a Method* by Gordon R. Sullivan and Michael V. Harper (Broadway Books, 1993). It was written by two army generals and its point is that you can *hope* for things to happen or you can *plan* for them to happen. Hope will only get you so far.

Are Your Goals Realistic?

Now, let me slightly contradict that last thought regarding big goals. Goals must also be realistic. Are you familiar with the legend of Achilles and the term *Achilles's heel?*

According to the *New World Encyclopedia*:

> In Greek mythology, Achilles was the hero of the Trojan War, the greatest of all the Greek warriors, and is the central character of Homer's *Iliad.*

No, they're not talking about Brad Pitt. The *New World Encyclopedia* continues:

> Achilles' most notable feat during the Trojan War was the slaying of the Trojan prince Hector outside the gates of Troy as they battled one another. Achilles was speculated to have been killed near the end of the Trojan War by Paris, who shot him in the heel with an arrow . . .[9]

> Later legends . . . state that Achilles was invulnerable in all his body except for his heel . . . Alluding to these legends, the term "Achilles' heel" has come to mean a point of weakness.[10]

---

9 wikipedia.org/wiki/Achilles
10 newworldencyclopedia.org/entry/Achilles

Achilles was nearly invincible, but not in the one area where he was injured. We all have these vulnerable features. It is good to know yours.

Goals have vulnerabilities too. I know I just recommended setting huge goals, but you must also keep them realistic. For example, breathing in space without a respiration device is not physically possible, but breathing in space with one is. Goals need to be realistic. Breathing in space was a huge goal in early space travel, and it was achieved by scientists using realistic strategies. Reaching this goal made possible the vision of reaching the moon.

Determine whether you have the ability and the physical requirements for your goals. Are there are skills that need to be attained to achieve your goals? Take into account any limitations you may have to work with that could make the journey longer or force you to make adjustments along the way.

Set Deadlines for Your Goals

Goals should be easily measureable, so deadlines are crucial for goal setting. If you've given yourself five years to achieve a large goal, divide that time frame in half and then into increments to achieve smaller goals that will lead up to your larger goal. I subscribe to the belief that ninety days is too long. Too much can change in ninety days.

Divide big jobs into multiple goals that lead up to the final goal. For example, I set the tasks it would take to complete this book within a reasonable time, giving myself to the end of the first quarter of 2020. I started writing and revising this book in August of 2019. That gave me six months. Because that is more than ninety days, I broke down the book into chapters. I knew which ones I wanted done within ninety days. I came up with my smaller goals and set deadlines for them. Finally, I figured out how much time I wanted for rewrites and revisions. I set the final deadline to be the end of March of 2020, and backed that into my book outline.

Now, don't be afraid to adjust your timetable, but be sure to analyze why you are adjusting a deadline. Is it for a justifiable reason, or is it just because you are lazy? Sometimes you must make changes to account for an unforeseen obstacle. Adjust your timeline as necessary to move past challenges. Always keep your vision in front of you to keep you motivated.

Your Goals May Need to Change Along the Way

Today creates tomorrow. Every action you take today helps to create your future. Ask yourself if any of your habits could be an obstacle to reaching your goals. For instance, you may dream about retiring early and running a luxury spa in a beautiful location. However, if you lack the productive habit of keeping account of your daily expenses, you may find it challenging to save money to realize your goal.

Your Daily Routine Can Help You Move Toward Goals

Your daily routine should be designed to move you toward your goals. Decide on the things you'll do each day to achieve your smaller goals. For example, I try to write every day.

Once you've divided your lifetime goals into smaller ones, you may find yourself feeling overwhelmed, but all you need to do is prioritize your intermediate goals and keep them practical and achievable. Writing down your goals will help clarify them. Reading them will also remind you of your goals when life is trying to distract you.

There are obstacles to creating new habits and behavioral patterns, and the biggest obstacle is ourselves. Try to figure out the external and internal obstacles that may be in your way. For example, if you've decided that you're going to eat a healthy breakfast every day, get rid of all the breakfast junk food in your pantry and freezer. That junk food is an obstacle to successfully implementing your habit.

The obstacle might be time interference. Maybe your partner doesn't leave you alone for thirty minutes every night so you can meditate, write, read, or whatever it is you want to do toward your goal. Simply let them know ahead of time that you need to be undisturbed during this time. This could even save a relationship. I have a home office and a downtown office so I can bifurcate family and work time.

Sometimes those close to you may find it challenging to understand why you're working so hard to achieve your goals.

They mean well, but they may be struggling with their own goals. This could manifest in words and actions you may find discouraging. Jealousy is another possibility. Just be aware of these realities and keep a positive outlook on your journey.

Do Not Become Disheartened by Obstacles

Be prepared to flow with the changes in your life. Stay in sync with the universal flow, and life will run much more smoothly. The only constant in life is change.

As you grow older, your priorities may change. What you wanted to achieve years ago may be less important today. It's a good idea to review your goals from time to time. Choose the goals that are most important to you now. Put yourself in control of the changes ahead. Reaching your goals is as much fueled by your attitude as your work.

Determine how you can make a goal easier to achieve. While some amount of sacrifice will be involved, your overall journey should be a pleasure as you look forward to the attainment of your dreams. One way of keeping enthusiasm up is to reward yourself along the way. Even telling a supportive friend about a small achievement provides a sweet reward in the pride you feel. Maybe you could chart your progress and keep the chart where you'll see it every day.

Get Support

Let other know your goals. If other people are involved in the achievement of your goal, or if it's going to affect them, tell them about it so they may support you in your endeavors. If you need their help, let them know.

Surround yourself with others who have similar goals. CEOs do this all the time. Not only do they often have a board of directors, but they also have advisors. Some of these people may be their predecessors. Past presidents will often help to advise a current president, regardless of party lines.

If you're a writer with the goal of getting published, you could join a writer's workshop. If you'd like to become a golf champion, join a golf club. An aspiring artist could live in an artists' community for inspiration and support.

All of us have a hero within us, waiting to be discovered. Effectively setting goals that matter can lead you to becoming the best you can be and can bring you closer to enjoying the happy life you deserve.

Goal Setting

The *Balanced Scorecard* system, discussed on page 37, is great for this next exercise.

For this exercise, we will be focusing on the goal-setting or *developing initiatives* piece of the process.

To practice setting goals, let's use a real estate team example with these vision and mission statements:

- **Vision:** *Create exceptional lives through the right real estate.*

- **Mission:** *Be the preferred provider of real estate services in area X by delivering exceptional attention to client's budget, expert market knowledge, the best affiliate service providers, and matching lifestyle needs to real estate for our clients.*

Let's set goals for the coming year:

1. By the end of the first quarter, add three new buyer agents who have sold over $4 million.

2. By March of this year, install a new market analysis system that keeps clients up to date with all market trends for their specific needs.

3. Become known as experts in our market by achieving $20 million in sales in area X by year's end.

As you can see, the goals or initiatives are measurable, specific, and tied to the vision and mission. These goals can be assigned to a team member if need be. This can be applied to your life as well. Let's use a personal example:

- **Vision:** *Become the most exceptional HR professional in my company.*

- **Mission:** *Display the best technical and personal HR service for my clients by becoming known as an expert in my area, as well as a respected professional by employees inside and outside of my area.*

Goals for the coming year:

- Gain the technical knowledge to be PHR-certified by midyear.

- Meet with all employees in my service area at least once by year's end.

- Create a database of people whom I need to follow up with more often.

- Develop a tool for leadership so they can be more in tune to their people needs by March.

Goals can be spiritual in nature. I have a vision and mission to not only be a good leader for my family and community, but also be in a close relationship with my creator. I could set goals that are specific, measurable, trackable, and connected to that vision and mission. However, without setting these goals, how successful do you think I would be by just winging it?

Lead Activity: Practice Goal Setting

Take some time here to write your vision and mission again and then set some goals. You don't have to set all of them; just practice writing a few.

Keep working toward accomplishing your goals even if life throws more than a few obstacles at you. Know what you're after as the *CEO for Life* and stay focused. Make your goals a part of your daily life and use positive affirmations. Acknowledge what you've done to keep moving forward. Apply these strategies consistently to help you meet your *CEO for Life* goals.

Practice Goal Setting

Practice Goal Setting

Chapter 5

Values – Never Sacrifice Who You Are

Your beliefs become your thoughts, your thoughts become your words, your words become your actions, your actions become your habits, your habits become your values, your values become your destiny.

~ Unknown

Would you ever drink water from a muddy stream? Of course not; you would drink filtered water. Sometimes you might pay as much as five dollars for a bottle of filtered water.

Let's talk about the filters you are applying to your life as the CEO. Values are a set of filters. Think of them as a mosquito net around the vision and mission. It not only keeps out the unwanted, but also finely filters your decision-making process. It is a layer of protection to ensure you make the right decisions to support your vision and mission.

When it comes to your vision and mission, values are like a mosquito net; they not only keep the good stuff in, but also keep out the bugs that want to get in. What do I mean by *bugs?* Bugs can be goals you set that are not in alignment with your culture, or your internal compass. Bugs are factors that might allow you to make less-than-ethical decisions within your goals.

You have to make decisions every day as the *CEO for Life.* If your goals are not protected by values, you can make some crappy decisions. Decisions that are not in alignment will eventually lead you astray from where you want to be.

I have read that if you were off by one degree when you launched a rocket going to the moon, you would end up 4,169 miles off. That is almost twice the diameter of the moon.[11] Now I am thinking of all of you reading this book as aspiring astronauts. Your values will keep your course correct.

Being in HR for a Fortune 150 company for thirteen years, I saw some of the best people make decisions that were unethical, immoral, and downright surprising. No matter how well they had their goals set, with vision and mission ingrained, they would falter because of values. As an entrepreneur in the commercial and real estate space, I saw it ten times more. The added pressure of making deals happen, with commission-based incentives, created the perfect storm for values to be thrown out the window.

---

11 christoculture.com/blog/the-one-degree-difference

I saw people who were driven and goal-oriented, whose mission and vision were huge, but they eventually failed because of their values. I want this chapter to raise your antenna to the long game. Do not sacrifice who you are for the short game. Al Pacino gives a great speech in the 1999 movie, *Any Given Sunday*, in which his character says, "Life's this game of inches."[12] The long game is always the way to frame vision, mission, and goals. Your values help you keep everything structured correctly and aligned.

Morals Versus Values as *CEO for Life*

From time to time, my clients—especially those who feel intense pressure to make things happen in life and professionally—ask me about the difference between morals and ethics.

I always ask them, "What do you think you should do?"

Then I follow immediately with, "Let me rephrase; what do you *feel* you should do?"

Most everyone has an internal compass that knows what the right decision is. It always happens the same way. They give a long pause. Their eyes shift or they shift in their seat. Then they say, "I know." They just needed to be reminded.

Let's unpack for a moment what morals and values are.

---

12 youtu.be/_b7bgtu2O4E at 1:50 mark

This quote, by an Irish novelist and an Anglican clergyman from the 1700s, helps me discern the difference between the two.

> *Respect for ourselves guides our morals;*
> *respect for others guides our manners.*
> ~ Laurence Sterne, novelist

I actually adapt it a little:

> *Respect for ourselves guides our morals;*
> *respect for others guides our values.*

A value is an outward expression of our morals. Morals are the basis for our values. Hence, they are a filter. They work hand in hand. Values are the actionable manifestation of your morals.

Personal Values

When developing your values, I recommend you use no more than five brief statements. They might be just a single word.

I mentioned earlier that we are building a finely tuned timepiece to be the best *CEO for Life*. In that finely tuned timepiece is precision, thought, careful craftsmanship, and the knowledge that no matter how small a spring or gear may be, it has its role that is critical to the whole. Remember, you are reading this for *your* CEO course, not mine, or anyone else's.

A side note: Do not place your values on others; you will be let down. Be the example. At the same time, make your values yours. Living a life built upon values takes courage.

Here is a list of common values that many companies use. They also apply to you as *CEO for Life*.

- Integrity (ethics, honesty)
- Respect (trust, dignity)
- Excellence (quality, performance)
- Responsibility (accountability, commitment)
- Teamwork (collaboration, cooperation)
- Innovation (creativity, ingenuity)
- Achievement (results, success)
- Fairness (diversity, inclusive)
- Care (service, compassion)
- Passion (enthusiasm, fun)
- Leadership (influence, competitive advantage)
- Learning (continuous improvement, knowledge)
- Customers (customer satisfaction)
- People (employee engagement)
- Safety (health)
- Community (corporate citizenship)
- Environment (sustainability)[13]

---

13 Ferguson, Robert. *Developing Your Differentiating Values for Business: A Practical Guide for Creating Competitive Advantage in Business.* Ferguson Values. fergusonvalues.com/developing-your-differentiating-values/

Here is an excellent exercise to self-reflect and build out your values.

Discovery Activity: Self-Reflection Questions:

---

1. What are my values? Can others figure out my values by the way I live my life?

2. Looking back on my last major decision, do I see how my values guided me?

3. How would my life change if I wrote out my values, shared them with people, and lived by my values? Would my life improve or get worse?

4. In what ways do I live life with courage?

5. Would consistency in practicing my values with courage make a difference?

6. Why is living with courage important?

7. What areas of my life can I step up more with courage as they relate to living my values?

8. Do I celebrate that I have values and they are all mine?

9. Do you have the courage to limit the people around you who do not share your values?

Self-Reflection Questions:

Self-Reflection Questions:

Chapter 6

Hiring and Firing as *CEO for Life*

Even if you cannot change all the people around you,
you can change the people you choose to be around. Life
is too short to waste your time on people who don't
respect, appreciate, and value you. Spend your life with
people who make you smile, laugh, and feel loved.
~ Roy T. Bennett, *The Light in the Heart*

Discovery Activity: Assess Your Surroundings

Name three people who are not helping you right now to be the best version of you. Write them down below. And don't fudge this.

1.

2.

3.

If you were not willing to write their name here, you are not serious about refining your circle for success. Recognize that. The best vision, mission, goals, and values won't matter unless you get this right. Again, a *CEO for Life* characteristic is being discerning about the people you surround yourself with.

Who Are You?

Jim Rohn famously said, "You're the average of the five people you spend the most time with."

In my life, I boiled it down to three physical relationships outside of family. We are in a new connection era. You are probably connected and being fed by hundreds of people via social media. We have few daily physical interactions compared with our digital interactions. The influence circle, face to face, has gotten smaller and more important. I am not bashing social media in any way. Social media interactions are critical for networking and exploring ideas. Having a large digital net to connect with is a good idea.

For example, I met two incredible, influential people via a Zoom call because I reached out to them on LinkedIn. They reviewed my profile, video, and posts and agreed to spend time with me, and now we are engaging on projects together. I appreciate the expertise of these thought leaders, but I still keep a tight grip on my interactions and how much influence people have on me.

Hiring and Firing

A long time ago, I was taught important lessons on the job as the HR executive responsible for designing and executing the staffing, ensuring the right players remained for power plants in twenty-six states. Working this kind of job, you gain almost a sixth sense about people. Just like an athlete who has practiced a particular play—motion, exercise, swing—muscle memory is built. Instinct is fine-tuned.

The same goes for being the *CEO for Life*, whether you are in the workplace or life-place. Some firings are just obvious. The person who brings a gun to work to intimidate a colleague at lunch needs to be fired. The employee who calls the senior vice-president's phone every night and plays the violin needs to be fired. The executive who is monitored spending over 80 percent of their workday on porn sites needs to be fired. The employees having sex in the bathroom need to be fired. The family member who has nothing but negative defeating comments about your dreams needs to be fired. The boyfriend or girlfriend cheating on you needs to be fired. The best friend who is stealing money from you needs to be fired. The church that is not feeding you spiritually may not be the right place for you.

Who Are My Shareholders?

So how does this relate to both personal and professional life? The simple rule I use is to identify my shareholders.

If you are a *CEO for Life*, the people you surround yourself with are your shareholders. Not only are they investing in you because they believe in you, but they also believe that you have value. You give your shareholders equity in your life.

We all have heard the saying: *The rising tide lifts all boats.* Well, if a person is not lifting you up, then questions need to be asked. Anyone who is not a positive influence on getting me closer to my vision needs to be released from my life or the workplace. They will draw energy that could be better used. Time that could be better used. Brain power that could be better used.

Choosing quality shareholders will protect you from going outside the guardrails we talked about earlier. I bet you are thinking: *Well, this sounds selfish.* And it is. A good selfish. If you are not the best *CEO for Life*, how can you be the best for those around you? You will hurt those you care about or work with by not being your best.

> *You cannot live the best life with the worst people.*
> ~ Robert Barber, CHPC

Let's look at the *CEO for Life* as if you were building an organization. Ask the question, "Whom do I need to surround myself with to reach my vision?"

I spent seven years traveling the country to some of the most remote places to build organizations with a focus on making electrons—the energy business. I love the thought now because it's an analogy for my life. I want to energize people.

Consider this scenario:

You arrive in rural Iowa and the employment rate is awful, skill level is medium, and the poverty level is high. It would be easy to hire those you can and collect your check. Or you can go through the process of knowing you have been entrusted with billions of dollars of investment and need to build a team that will succeed.

You want the people to succeed. You must make difficult decisions, tell some people no, and invest in people who are better aligned. You may have to stretch yourself to surround yourself with people who share your vision.

People. That's how, while I was in corporate, we grew from two states to twenty-six states and over three thousand employees, and we attained a stock price that was beyond expectation. People become your shareholders. They invest not in the stock, but in the vision, mission, goals, and values. Shareholders in your life are the same. The process is hard because you will want to care for people, give chances, and make excuses, but those behaviors will not serve your vision.

Sometimes you need to fire even yourself. I always start out with an inventory of my strengths. Then I seek out who can enhance my strengths. I look for the necessary positions as my company grows, whether it is someone to oversee finance, HR, technology, production, operations, or customer service.

> *Lead Activity: Prioritize your shareholder list in order of those with the biggest impact on your vision to those with the least impact:*

1.

2.

3.

4.

5.

It may feel funny ranking people, but face it: There are some people lifting you up more than others. It is smart to be mindful of this order when you are managing how your time is being spent.

At this point, I am always asked, "Can I keep some of my shareholders or help them?" At a minimum, limit exposure or time with anyone who is not lifting or elevating you to your vision. When trimming down the shareholders as the *CEO for Life*, you are not always able to fully cut people out. The answer is Control/Not Control. Each of us is only asked to be the best we can, because that is what we can control. You do not have control over the outcomes of the behaviors of your shareholders, just the position they hold in your life as *CEO for Life*.

Chapter 7

Learn to Love "No"

If you want more time, freedom, and energy,
start saying no.

~ Anonymous

There was a Huffpost article that was written some time ago, entitled "No Is Not a Bad Word."[14] This article, along with another book I read about setting boundaries, changed everything for me. The funny thing is that my business partner for the last thirteen years was a ninja at this *CEO for Life* practice. He was so highly skilled and disciplined that he was not afraid of no. In fact, he saw it as an absolute necessity to success. Every *CEO for Life* will be bombarded with activities, tasks, and people who want to pull you in different directions with challenges that are not really issues. You need to be super disciplined with no. *No I will not let that distract me; No, that can wait; No, that is not important right now.*

---

14 huffpost.com/entry/no-is-not-a-bad-word_b_12731010

When I was in business for myself, I was the most stressed when I should have been the most relaxed. It was when we had the most business. Clients were seeking our services and money was rolling in. The company was growing, with sales over $900 million in real estate for the year; commission checks and distributions were unbelievable. But I was miserable.

Why? I had not learned the discipline of *no*.

Most of us start out in our workplace or life-place in a position of scarcity, meaning we are grinding to get where we want to go. We build this mentality of *I have to do it all, for as many as I can, for as long as I can.* That is a position of weakness if it becomes an obstacle. For me, it had. The faster our train went, the more I felt I needed to shovel the coal into the engine.

I answered every phone immediately, returned every voicemail, email, and text immediately, took every meeting or opportunity on someone else's terms, took on every client, or assignment. In simple terms, I had not set any boundaries for myself and had not learned the discipline of no. Nor that it was okay to say no.

Meanwhile, my business partners seemed to be calm, cool, and collected, not pushed around by their day. I mentioned earlier that I was given the book, *Boundaries: When to Say YES, When to Say NO, To Take Control of Your Life*, by my pastor (Zondervan, 1992). At the same time, my business partner—and best friend—sat me down and told me to start saying no.

This is a major *CEO for Life* skill. You would have thought that during the thirteen years I spent working with the highest level of executives, I would have caught on. These executives were always in control of their time. At first, saying no did not feel natural for me; I had to learn how to do it. I had to learn to control my time and not let circumstances or others determine for me how my day would run.

Saying no is a skill. It doesn't mean that you don't care about a person or topic or that you feel superior, it's about prioritizing what is important right then and realizing that most of what comes at us each day will resolve itself with time.

It used to drive me crazy when my one partner would wait to return calls and emails. One day we talked about it, and he said that 99 percent of what is coming at you will resolve itself. The trick is to sift through to identify the 1 percent and attack that.

So, let me ask you: right now, what are you saying yes to that you should be saying no to?

| *Lead Activity: The Art of Saying No and Setting Boundaries.* |

Ask yourself: *What is getting me closer to my vision for my life? What habits are getting me closer? What relationships are getting me closer?*

Think about how you spend your day: *Do you really need two hours in the gym in the morning and at night? Do you need to be at every happy hour? How important is watching* Game of Thrones *for the third time? Do you really need that client that you know in your heart is only using you and will never amount to a payday? How many times are you going to try to convince a prospect who has told you now for three years that they need you?*

Let's make a list for setting boundaries right now by answering some questions. Get your pen ready.

1. Can I say, "No more."?

2. What keeps me from saying no or setting boundaries?

3. What boundaries do I need to work on in my workplace or life-place?

4. What is draining me the most every day that I can either delegate or just stop altogether?

5. Which leads can be sold on my vision or my product? What leads do I need to pass on and move on to more yeses?

6. What relationships or habits may need to be dialed back for better focus?

7. How much more focus do I feel I would have if I gave myself permission to take control of my time?

Chapter 8

Self-Development: Focus on Your Strengths

Focus on your strengths, not your weaknesses. Focus on your character, not your reputation. Focus on your blessings, not your misfortunes.
~ Roy T. Bennett, *The Light in the Heart*

I am currently forty-eight years old and I'm still taking classes and learning. I know there are plenty of voices that advise, "Just go out and do it," without taking classes. I get it. However, you can do both. Don't hesitate to take on formal learning from other experts to put more tools in the shed. I love Udemy.com, a site that specializes in online video courses you can use to expand your skillset. By learning and then doing it yourself, you gain expertise.

When I was in real estate, it would frustrate my partner that I needed to know every piece of the buy-sell process. I mean I really wanted to *know* it. I wanted to know title, mortgages, inspections, construction—all of it—even though it was not required or expected of my role in a deal. I felt the more I knew, the better I could serve, and the more successful I would be. I did not get licensed in all these disciplines, but I wanted to know the basics. I wanted to know what to look out for, and know the risk points and the advantage points for my clients.

The same goes for my coaching business. Did I need to get certified by the High Performance Institute or get the other skills I have acquired to be successful? Probably not, but they make me better and more confident in the services I deliver. There are a million and one ways to build your skills, self-develop, and get better. The point is that it is not enough to sit back and just think you know it all and allow your ego to lull you into submission.

Can I be a better dad? Yes, sir. Can I be a better husband? Darn right. Can I be a better consultant? Yes. Do those whom I serve as the *CEO for Life* deserve my best? Damn right.

So, what are some ways to improve? Certifications, classes, reading, and habits are some ideas. Take baby steps. Pick only the things that you know you will complete, practice, and fully focus on. It may be only one thing this year. That's okay. As long as self-development is always a part of your *CEO for Life* game plan.

This chapter's main theme may be a bit contrarian, but it goes back to an underlying theme in this book, which is that *you only have so much time.* I can make only one promise in this book with a 100 percent guarantee: *You will die.* Time will run out, so spend it wisely.

Strengths and Weaknesses

This leads me to the main point. Should you focus on your strengths or weaknesses?

Peter Drucker has the shortest and best book on this subject called *Managing Oneself* (Harvard press, 2008).

Almost every performance appraisal system or formal development system says you should focus on developing your weaknesses into strengths. From the time we entered school, we were all asked to focus on working on our weaknesses. I would suggest you don't have time for this as *CEO for Life.* The most successful people I have met in my life only focus on their strengths.

It seems counterintuitive. I liken it to football. You don't put a lineman as a cornerback or vice versa. They are slotted to play for their strengths. Now can they improve those strengths? Absolutely. But there are others who have been put on the team to fill in gaps or weaknesses.

Here's an example from my life that shows the advantage of focusing on strengths: When I left college to go to work, I went into my discipline as an electrical engineer. Within just three years, it became apparent to me that although I had good skills, I was never going to be a great engineer. I began to assess my strengths. I was logical, great at solving problems, and I loved people. When I realized this, I applied for the first HR position I could find in the company. I was told by the interviewing director that engineers do not make good HR people. Well, let's say I proved that thesis completely wrong.

Discovery Activity: Strengths and Weaknesses

Take a moment and assess your strengths and weaknesses below. Write out your top three strengths and top three weaknesses. Then start thinking about how you can develop your strengths for the workplace or life-place. As for the weaknesses, figure out how to delegate them, hire them out, or give them away to someone better.

Strengths

1.

2.

3.

Weaknesses

1.

2.

3.

I am not a *details* person overall. I can be, but I like to be four steps ahead in my thinking and efforts. At home, these characteristics do not lend themselves to bill paying. My wife, on the other hand, runs our house from three calendars. She knows down to the minute what task is in the works and what comes next, and she runs our family like the captain of the USS Roosevelt. Flawlessly. We are both highly skilled, but we have different skills. We complement each other because we know each other's strengths and play to them well.

Self-Development Through Journaling

You may ask me, "So Rob, what are some things that I should be doing in the area of self-development?"

We will explore a bunch of ideas next, but let's unpack a big one. I am a big believer in journaling when starting a self-development journey. During my life, journaling has been a critical piece of my strategy.

How does journaling help you with self-development?

Journaling is a fantastic way to supercharge your self-development efforts. In *Managing Oneself*, Drucker offers the concept of feedback analysis. Over a period of time, you journal your desired outcomes, how you did, and what contributed to your success or failure. Over time, you will find common threads to your successes and your strengths.

Journal when thoughts are fresh. When thoughts are new in your mind, they can be challenging to analyze objectively.

I find thoughts or ideas often need to sit and marinate. In your head, an idea may feel like a winner, but after writing it out and thinking about it, your idea may turn out to be *WWIT (What was I thinking?)*. Putting things down on paper provides a totally different perspective.

Thinking happens to be linear for most people; one thought leads to the next, which leads to the next. We often allow wishful thinking to enter into these sequences. We think to ourselves: *How could this not work? This will lead to this, and then this, and then this.*

Journaling gives you the ability to see things from outside of your head, to get a perspective view away from the brain's noisy and distracted environment. Journaling helps me solve complex challenges just as it did in my engineering days. I constantly write ideas down as it helps me see patterns and reorganize. I tell my children to use all the scratch paper they need when they are working on a problem. It is so beneficial to write things out. When you write on paper, the solution to a complex obstacle may suddenly become obvious.

Journaling, even though may not feel natural for you now, is a skill that will increase clarity. The practice of journaling helps you map your progress. Sometimes we feel like we're not getting anywhere, when in fact we have moved further than we give ourselves credit for. Remember, we are conditioned with a sense of *We cannot make progress*. When you're feeling this way, go back and review your old journal. You'll be amazed at how much progress you've made.

People often fear journaling for the same reason many professionals do not vlog or podcast. They are filled with self-doubt. *What could I have to say that is important enough to write down?* Even if you think that you have no important thoughts, you are wrong. You are here on purpose. It is worth writing about your dreams and keeping track of your progress and the way you surmount obstacles that come your way. Set a reminder or alarm daily to remind you to journal for five to fifteen minutes. You spend more time in the bathroom. Even getting down a couple of sentences on a regular basis can make all the difference. You'll be surprised how often you'll write much more.

Lead Activity: Start Journaling Today

1. Pick a time of day when you will commit to journaling.

2. Decide how you will journal: handwriting, typing, on your phone or computer, in a book?

3. Always review your journal entries at least once a week.

Remember, this is an investment in you. This should be an activity you want to do.

Other Self-Development Ideas

Remember, you only get rewards from those things you practice consistently. Let's discuss some other ideas that can get you off to the races.

I liken these practices to a *leads database*. Many of the people I consult for are in sales of some type. The first thing I say to them is, "Tell me about your process for collecting and systematically managing leads."

Nine times out of ten, they don't even have a database. I then ask, "How many contacts do you have in your phone and email?"

Hundreds. I shake my head. Inevitably, they ask me what I use. I tell them it doesn't matter what I use. I use what works for me. I tell them to pick a method that they will use. You cannot imagine how many people's businesses have turned around from just making that one change.

The first idea we've discussed is to keep a journal. Here are some other ideas to assist with self-development:

- Move your body. Jeff Bezos and Elon Musk take long walks each day.

- Call your parents and ask them for input on your strengths and weaknesses.

- Play with your kids. This is always a good idea. I learn a ton from my teenagers.

- Practice effective money management. Hire a CFO for your life. If you don't have an accountant or at least a financial advisor, get one!

- Read. The written word is powerful.

- Join an activity club. I have a men's group that meets Thursdays. I serve at my church and was an elder for several years, which was amazing for my growth.

- Do daily affirmations. Some people feel funny about these, but they work. What you feed your mind also feeds your heart and soul.

- Delve into a subject of interest. Dive in.

- Visit a school nearby and offer your services. Adjunct a class.

- Admiral William H. McRaven suggests: "If you want to change the world, start off by making your bed."[15]

- Try a new hobby. I recently started hiking three days a week and I'm loving it.

- Volunteer a few hours of your time each week.

- Do something that scares you each day.

---

15 From Admiral McRaven's commencement address to the graduates of The University of Texas at Austin on May 17, 2014. news.utexas. edu/2014/05/16/mcraven-urges-graduates-to-find-courage-to-change-the-world/

- Learn a new language.

- Take a Udemy class.

- Start a blog. Write.

- Learning how to meditate can be wonderful. I suggest Jaggi Sadhguru, yogi, author, and meditation expert.

- Take a trip to someplace new. It always helps me grow when I get out of my little geographical bubble.

- Join your Chamber of Commerce. Get to know what is going on in your community.

The most important thing about starting the self-development journey is to not to self-sabotage. What does that mean? Don't allow excuses to get in the way of your growth.

Discovery Activity:
Self-Reflection: Fending Off Self-Sabotage

Here are some questions to ask yourself.

1. Do people who matter, *including me*, support my taking on this self-development activity?

2. What is my time commitment? You must set a calendar or schedule.

3. What will I do to stay on track this time? [If you have gotten off track in the past]

4. What forces may stop me from self-development? Which can I control?

5. Will someone else benefit from me doing this? (This is a powerful question.)

6. Will I regret in a year that I did not start today?

7. Will this reinforce my strengths?

Consider the questions you ask yourself on a regular basis. When you ask yourself effective questions, you'll get the answers you need. Focus on your strengths and make a plan to do something, then commit to it, and grow.

Chapter 9

Firefighting: Prepare Today for the Fire Tomorrow

Tomorrow's victory is today's practice.
~ Chris Bradford, The Way of the Warrior

As *CEO for Life*, you will be tested. It is easy to be calm, cool, and collected when all is well and right with the world. Guess what? It will not always be this way.

This reminds me of the Old Testament story of Shadrach, Meshach, and Abednego. They had been enslaved in servitude in King Nebuchadnezzar's rule, but in cushy roles in a palace. Regardless of what was asked of them, they would serve, but never at the sacrifice of their faith. This resulted in them being thrown into a fiery furnace, one so hot that even the guards outside were burned alive.

But these three had strengthened their faith with continual practice every day. They were prepared for any firestorm that came forth. In this account, a fourth being appeared in the fire to keep them unharmed, and they were spared by their faith. Regardless of your faith or belief system, this is still a powerful picture of how you need to perform as *CEO for Life*. You must prepare yourself daily for the firestorm you will encounter.

What do you think the number two job of a CEO may be, after setting vision, mission, goals, and culture?

It is fighting fires. Most days it will feel like job number one. It may already seem like your number one role. Accept it. Don't run from it or complain about it. Every serious fire will be coming to you, because you are the *CEO for Life*.

I live my life in three major stages daily.

1. I am in a fire

2. I am coming out of a fire.

3. I am going into a fire.

That is an effective way to sum up life. Why? Because it frames a *be prepared* mindset that allows you to stay on offense, not defense. You can't enter a weightlifting contest and only go to the gym the day before, or enter a sculpting competition and learn sculpting from a YouTube video that same morning. You will not be ready.

Now do not get this mixed up. I am not asking you to come from a position of fear or anxiety. You must come from a position of *conscious offense* to be prepared for the fires that will come. To be prepared as the *CEO for Life* is to be ready for fighting fires.

When I was in the real estate business, I learned that the day-to-day experience could be broken down into two main categories: *marketing* and *firefighting*. The marketing piece is easy to see. The firefighting is where your realtor will show if they are worth their salt as a professional. It is where the realtor makes their money. Every real estate deal has obstacles because it can be emotional; it is a deal and negotiation process, it involves a lot of money, laws, and regulations, and there are several hands on the process from the beginning to end.

We learned to make sure we had time to hit the pause button on fires that could happen. It's okay to walk away from some fires or ask for help. A good *CEO for Life* knows when to call for backup. *Fire vacation* was a term my business partner and I came up with to describe the need for a break in the firefighting.

Growth Happens in the Valley

I went to breakfast one day with an advisor and great friend of mine. It was one of our regularly scheduled times to pour our thoughts into one another. We got on the topic of the mountaintops and the valleys of life.

He asked me, "Why do we need both in life?"

I responded, "Because we need the perspective of difference."

He then unleashed on me a game changer in workplace and life-place by asking me the question, "Why don't trees—or much else—grow on mountaintops?"

I said I didn't know.

Then he said, "The only growth happens in the valley."

And it made perfect sense. On the mountaintop, we stay for short times. The view is amazing, but very little can grow there. Atmosphere and conditions don't allow for growth. In contrast, in the valley everything grows, the animals feed, and all the living things reproduce.

Growth happens in the valley.

Your firefighting will happen in the valley also. You will journey as *CEO for Life* into valleys where you will find fires. Know this, and know that it is a blessing. You may say, "Blessing? What?" Yes, it is a blessing. It is an opportunity for growth.

The moral of the story is when you decide to be the *CEO for Life* you will face challenges, decisions, mistakes, and tough times, but you will be in growth mode. The valley is where you grow. Never run from fires. Be the firefighter. Know that role in both workplace and life-place. Not everyone will run in, but you will be prepared because of this book and thesis. Firefighting is part of being *CEO for Life*.

Firefighting as the *CEO for Life*

The three steps to firefighting as *CEO for Life* are:

- Preparation
- Identification
- Resolution

Preparation

Every chapter leading up to this is part of your preparation for firefighting. Your vision, your mission, goals, and values all set in motion your preparation for handling the fires that will come.

I remember my first big firefight as an HR executive. We had been building power plants and renewable energy sites across the country. Our little-known company was finally getting some good attention and people wanted to come work for us. We also attracted a lot of attention that was contrary to the culture we were building. We began to attract employees who said they were buying into our culture, but it became very clear that some employees, as well as the leadership, would say one thing, but would march to a different beat when they wanted.

A clash of culture was coming to a head as performance declined, employees began to cut corners, and leadership would speak out of both sides of their mouths. However, we were prepared for this firefight because we had set a firm vision with a great buy-in, we had developed a clear mission, we had set and achieved goals, and we had a culture built on people values.

This is why I push for you to make good preparations now.

To expect the unexpected
shows a thoroughly modern intellect.
~ Oscar Wilde

Another example of being prepared is in the movie *Ants*. I love this movie. It is a perfect depiction of being prepared. If you have not seen the movie, a colony of ants spends the entire year preparing for winter. Every ant has a job and role in that preparation. Meanwhile, the grasshoppers never prepare. They have always taken advantage of the ant's preparation. I won't give away the movie if you have not seen it, but preparation is the better idea.

Before anything else, preparation is the key to success.
~ Alexander Graham Bell

Identification

It isn't that they cannot find the solution.
It is that they cannot see the problem.
~ G. K. Chesterton, philosopher and writer

The next step is to identify the *right problem*. The right problem is the one at the center of the real issue. For example, I may not like my job, but my issue may be really that I do not like my boss. The real problem is found by asking a lot of "why" questions.

Boy, have I worked often with clients who have not asked enough questions to determine the right problem. As *CEO for Life* for workplace or life-place, you need to ask a lot of questions. I learned this skill from a mentor of mine, Jim Keener, whom I mention in the acknowledgements for this book. At the time, he was Vice President of Generation and I traveled the country with him. I was his chief *people person*. He was a huge proponent of the idea that the foundation of any great success story always started with the right people in alignment with one another. He cared tremendously for people.

What particularly amazed me about him was his operational skill of drilling down into a problem to its most simple form. We would have marathon problem-solving sessions at the plants where the question *"Why?"* was drilled over and over until we got to the simplest form of problem identification. I had never experienced such methodical problem identification. To this day, I carry an engineering notebook in which I document everything in excruciating detail to ensure I have the right information to work from.

If you want to be a great problem identifier, your best friend is the question "Why?" Keep asking until there are no more answers.

Resolution

A *CEO for Life* must be committed to seeing the problem resolved.

Being a Balanced Scorecard Professional, I love brainstorming. As a *CEO for Life*, you will find there is never just one right answer. There may need to be a set of answers to reach the desired resolution to the fire at hand. Sometimes, an answer may just float to the top, but in many cases, that's not it. Being a *CEO for Life* while wearing my "dad hat" has sometimes been difficult. *Timeout* was a simple answer when they were three-to-five years old, but now they are fifteen and twenty, and timeout is not the answer. There is no one answer to every problem. Often the answer is a set of steps and strategies with agreement and consensus, and it usually involves money. From what I am told, the money part never goes away when it comes to your kids.

Recently a fire came up about life direction for my oldest daughter. The decision was to continue to pursue school right now or enter the workforce in a field she was interested in. This presented many questions to consider, like where she would live, what job to pursue, what kind of budget she could manage, and when the transition would take place. As a family and team, we got together and brainstormed all these items to determine a strategy map. From there we could set forth a plan with goals and initiatives, just as a CEO would set forth for a new venture. We went through strengths, weaknesses, opportunities, and threats (SWOT) analysis. I am not kidding. Managing your life challenges as a *CEO for Life* will make the process easier and more streamlined.

Another example where the mentality of a *CEO for Life* made all the difference was the major life-place firestorm of losing my mom unexpectedly. In 2018, I awoke to a Sunday morning phone call that my mom had passed away on the way to the hospital. She was young and it was completely unexpected. My mother raised me as a single mom from the time she was seventeen. She dedicated her life to a better life for us both. There were no trust funds, alimony, or a father in the picture. It was just us. She taught me to be all that I am spiritually, as a person, parent, husband, and businessperson. She gave up her dream of being a fashion designer to become an RN to support us, and then turned that expertise into three very successful companies. Her loss shifted the ground beneath me.

As the *CEO for Life* of my life—as well as the lives of my family members—this loss set in motion an ordeal that made me feel like I was in the fiery furnace. It caused us to go back to our personal vision, mission, and goals to reevaluate. What did we even define as success? In the end, our family came out with a new vision, mission, and goals. The perspective caused us to reconsider our time and legacy, and many new decisions came out of this.

I decided to sell my equity position in our firm—with sales of $917 million in 2018—pick up our family and move to Chattanooga, Tennessee, somewhere we had said we would live one day, and start a new business as a business coach through which I could pour my life into others' success. My wife quit her job as a speech pathologist to spend more time with our children. We threw out what we currently called our life and asked, "What do we really want?" We adjusted our life to meet a new life that was more fulfilling. We achieved a new vision together.

Now, a mistake I see many new CEOs make is going it alone. Yes, the buck does stop with you. However, you do not have to make decisions or test alternatives in a vacuum. Ask for help. Do you think Elon Musk, Jeff Bezos, and Mark Cuban achieved their success by doing it alone? No. They asked for help. For example, Jeff Bezos' initial startup funding came from his parent's savings. He was not afraid to ask for help.

A major part of resolving is visualizing. If you cannot visualize the successful outcome, how can you motivate anyone else? Another facet is *stick-to-itiveness*—a word that a good friend of my dad's taught me. He said the word *perseverance* is overused and the word *stick-to-itiveness* felt stronger to him as a character trait. A person's success is directly correlated to their stick-to-itiveness. So many don't see the fruits of their work because they give up, sometimes just on the cusp of a breakthrough.

Finally, when the fire is over, debrief with a focus on how to avoid the same fire again. You know the saying, "The definition of insanity is doing the same thing over and over again, but expecting different results." Make sure you don't set yourself up for the same fires over and again. That is not very CEO-like.

Discovery Activity: Self-Reflection Questions

---

1. Recall a recent workplace or life-place "fire."

2. How could have the *CEO for Life* mentality have helped you?

3. Walk that same fire through the steps above and see how different the outcome could have been.

4. Will you commit to being prepared and preparing today for any fire that comes your way?

5. What will you commit to as preparation?

Self-Reflection Questions

Self-Reflection Questions

Self-Reflection Questions

Chapter 10

You Set the Tone

Doubt kills more dreams than failure ever will.
~ Suzy Kassem, poet and philosopher

So, as we round third base on this journey to know you as the *CEO for Life*, it is time to talk about how critical it is to *set the tone* of your life. That is different from what we talked about in the introduction regarding the need to get your thought process right. We are now talking *daily littles*, the small things that add up to the big things. These small things make up the tone of who you are.

I like to think of individual notes in a concert that make a full symphony. If your tone is *complainer*, *slammer*, or *finger-pointer*, then that is the song that will play out in your term as the *CEO for Life*. If you have *gratitude*, *seek joy*, and *put others first*, then those are the songs you will play. In addition, they are what you will attract.

Hum to yourself. Seriously, hum to yourself. That's your tone. You have a tone to your CEO life. Spend three times a day humming your tune to yourself. Set an alarm on your phone. Mine is "The Adventure" from *Angels & Airwaves*. I hum that all day. Thank you, Tom DeLonge and crew.

When it comes to setting the tone, what comes to mind are three main categories:

- Fear versus fierce
- Regret
- Servant mindset

I know it may seem like an unlikely trio. What does regret have to do with the servant mindset? Why are fear and fierce tied together?

They all impact your tone, so they are all tremendously important for setting your tone.

Regret is a sneaky emotion that builds on itself and is almost impossible to fix unless you get ahead of it. *Servant mindset* is the act of caring for another more than yourself. If you spend more time caring for others or putting others first, you will create an enormous tornado of happiness that will sustain your tone through even the toughest times. Then there is *fear* versus *fierce*. You can operate in either or both, and they are a reinforcement to your tone. Let's spend some time delving a bit deeper into each one of these pillars for setting your tone as the *CEO for Life*.

Don't be overheard complaining . . .
Not even to yourself.
~ Marcus Aurelius

Fear Versus Fierce

What I have found is that CEOs operate in an oscillation between *fear* and *fierce*. Those are two distinctly different tones to operate from, and often, they can be in parallel. Now most people seem to correlate fear with weakness, but fear helps you be present and maintain focus. It is how you use the emotion that is critical.

Was I afraid to sell out of my company, move my family, and start over again in an entirely new business at forty-eight years of age? Heck, yes. But I realized that I was too comfortable, and I know comfort can be a disease that can steal your life. I used the fear I felt to test my fortitude and commitment to the vision we had set ahead of us. With the fear came excitement and a sense of adventure.

Lead me, follow me, or get out of my way.
~ General George Patton

Then there is *fierce*. CEOs operate with a fierceness as well. This fierceness can keep words like *can't, won't, impossible,* and *never* from invading the gray space between their ears.

I am obsessed with lions. It's not that I want to own one as a pet; I just love studying them. I had a chance once while in Uganda to experience them up close in their own natural environment. I was forever hooked. What I love the most is the quiet fierceness they display—in their appearance, their swagger, their pack life, how they take care of one another, how they don't apologize for sleeping all day, and most of all how both the lion and lioness roar!

A *CEO for Life* must have an amount of fierceness. Have a willingness to take risks, be bold, and roar! You do not become king of the jungle by being cowardly and comfortable.

Discovery Activity:
Self-Reflection Questions About Fear versus Fierce

---

1. What does *fear* mean to you? What does *fierce* mean to you?

2. Can you write down a time when fear helped propel you forward?

3. Are there situations you can describe when you wanted to be fierce, but were not? Why?

Self-Reflection Questions About Fear versus Fierce

The Regret Bucket

The *Regret Bucket* is something I came up with a few years ago. Being now forty-eight, I started to feel the weight of some life regrets, spiritual regrets, and work regrets. I went to the hardware store and bought a small bucket and wrote the word "Regret Bucket" on it. That bucket sits on my desk. My thesis is that when my life ends I want that bucket to be as empty as possible.

You already have a few regrets, but there are ways to help ensure you have far fewer of them over the rest of your life. There are few things more tragic than looking back over your life and wishing you had lived a life that was dramatically different. Now is the time to seize control of your future. It is time to get proactive and go on the offense against regrets. You can live a life that will fill you with smiles rather than regret!

Try these techniques to set a tone of fierceness in your life and ensure an empty regret bucket:

- Make a list of everything you want to see and do in your lifetime.

- Focus. Many regrets are the result of failing to direct your life toward something specific. Make a decision and move forward with fierceness.

- Time is not your friend. Do you even know what you did today? What did you spend your time on? Was it what you wanted or what you were God-gifted for?

- Settling is not an option. Would you settle for a knee doctor when you needed brain surgery? No, you would not. We so often settle for things because it's easy and we are lazy. Are you ready to stop settling?

- Roar more. Lions and lionesses both roar. You can roar louder. Let the world know you are here.

- Laugh more, especially at yourself. If you have not found a way to make a fool of yourself during the day, then you are not trying hard enough.

- There's no such thing as risk, just risk not accounted for. Live a life that has calculated risks.

- Burn bridges. I don't mean relationships, but I do mean bridges that would allow you to go backward.

- Fear is the leading cause of a regret-filled life. Taming your fear is the most important step. Learn to be uncomfortable now, to avoid regret later.

You can live a life that leads to satisfaction instead of regret. Get started today.

Discovery Activity: Self-Reflection Questions – Regret

---

1. What is your biggest regret right now?

2. Why is this regret in your life still?

3. Knowing now you are your *CEO for Life*, what would you have done differently about the circumstances that led to this regret?

4. As the *CEO for Life*, do you have control of how many more regrets fill up your bucket? Why or why not?

Self-Reflection Questions – Regret

Self-Reflection Questions – Regret

Servant Leadership

The greatest example for me of servant leadership is Jesus Christ. Regardless of whether you believe he is God, it's hard to argue the impact he has had on the world. The entire Western business world calendar is built around the guy. I think it is worth studying his leadership.

John 13:1–17 depicts an example of what it is to serve others. In this story, Jesus washes his disciples' feet. At this particular time in history, it was customary to have a servant wash your feet as you entered a rich person's home. People wore sandals and the streets were dusty and dirty. At this time, the disciples have entered to eat supper with Jesus, but there was no one to wash their feet. Jesus took it upon himself to show that he was not above anyone. The greatest thing someone in a position of leadership can do is serve those he serves with.

After setting an example, Jesus instructs his disciples:

> *If I then, your Lord and Teacher, have washed your feet, you also ought to wash one another's feet. For I have given you an example that you should do as I have done to you.*
> ~ John 13:14, KJV

This picture of serving has always been a motivator for me, especially when I think of the context of time and culture. For a teacher or leader to take on the task of washing his follower's feet, the impact is tenfold. Whose feet would you wash?

Being a servant lies between fear and fierce. It is a fearful thing to give someone else power and at the same time a mighty bold and fierce move to serve. New leaders may be fearful to give the appearance of servant leadership. I remember first leading people in corporate America. I felt like I had to be this big shot at first, but I quickly saw that the more successfully I helped my people, the more successful I became. The less I talked about me and the more I talked about my team, the better we did together. The more I celebrated them, the more they wanted to do for the team.

I will never forget my first real encounter with servant leadership, at least my first recognition of it. After high school, I went to a military college, Valley Forge Military College. While I was there, I was in the Pennsylvania National Guard. One weekend, we were going on a deployment that would have us in the woods the entire weekend on recon work in the middle of winter.

I thought I had my heavy outer gear, but when we arrived on base, I realized I was missing it. My sergeant major gave me his outer gear to wear for the weekend. He sacrificed his comfort and winter protection for one of his men. It probably seemed like a small thing to him, and I got some hazing for it, but it meant the world to me. From that day, I would have done anything to serve that guy. The military is a great example of servant leaders. As we were being trained to be officers, we were taught never to eat before the people we led. If there was nothing left to eat, that is the cost of leading.

Discovery Activity:
Self-Reflection Questions: Servant Leadership

---

1. Have you ever served someone at your expense?

2. Who has been a good example of servant leadership in your life?

3. Do you think you would achieve more with servant leadership or a dictatorship?

4. What can you do more of to reinforce your skill as servant leader in the workplace and life-place?

This chapter is designed to get you thinking about the tones you are putting out into the world and some of the basic tones of a *CEO for Life*. Your tones are creating a sheet of music for your life that others are listening to.

What do you want your tone to be, your tune to be, your influence to be?

Self-Reflection Questions: Servant Leadership

Self-Reflection Questions: Servant Leadership

Self-Reflection Questions: Servant Leadership

Conclusion

If you think you can or think you cannot, you are right.
~ attributed to Henry Ford

Do you have a friend in your life who has the ability to un-complicate everything you are trying to complicate? I have a great friend, John, who always breaks down our discussions. He is always telling me, "Rob, get out of your own way."

His view on life is that we overcomplicate everything. People need to have meetings to plan other meetings, but life can be much simpler. Recently, a small group I'm involved in had a study on the passage of John 16:23: "In that day you will ask Me nothing." I really sat with that for a long while.

We have so many questions, worries, anxieties. What if you just got out of your own way and got started?

My hope is that this book has sparked in you a new or renewed ownership of the way your life is lived. You cannot escape the fact you are the CEO of your life and it is for life. It really comes down to a question of how willing you are to embrace your place as *CEO for Life* and with what level of confidence and effort.

Oh, yeah, it takes effort, no matter your goals. It will take effort for the rest of your life.

I was once told *success* only comes before *work* in the dictionary. The same goes for you being the best version of *CEO for Life*.

If you don't deserve it, those around you do.

Next Steps

So what?

Have you asked that at all during your time reading this book? I hope so. I asked it a lot when I was writing it. I have an excellent friend who constantly pushes me to make sure if I put anything into the world, I ask that question first. People deserve more than just more noise and deserve the best from anyone that is going to put anything into the world.

So, what do you do with the information you have found in this book? What do you do now that you can no longer ignore you are the *CEO for Life?*

1. Tell people about the book and share your new job title and what it means.

2. If you want to take the book further with online breakdowns and exercises designed to be at your own pace. Visit ROYIacademy.com.

3. If you or your organization would like to book in-person training on this or other management concepts such as High Performance and Balanced Scorecard, or OKRs, connect with me at robebarber@royiacademy.com.

4. If you would like to book me for a speaking engagement, contact me at robertbarber@royiacademy.com or visit royiacademy.com/Speaking.

Case Studies

When I had finished the outline for CEO for Life, I thought it would be great to hear from real people—besides me—on this subject. So, I designed a set of questions and selected people I know and respect from different walks of life, ages, stages of life, and backgrounds. Some are successful in their own right, some are CEOs, and some, not.

I wanted to share the results with you to hit home these two ideas:

You are not alone in the process of being the CEO for Life.

You can start today.

SURVEY 1

My commentary:

What I found so intriguing in this set of responses was the question about what fires do they fight on a regular basis. The answer was "emotional." As you will see, this person has most of the CEO for Life map in place, but faces fires anyway, as you will. Firefighting will be mostly internal conflict, and you will need to be ready for it every day. Practicing how to overcome this conflict is critical to becoming the best CEO for Life.

1.   Do you have a personal vision and mission statement? Is it written down?

Yes, I have a personal mission statement, and yes, it's written down.

2.   How could you benefit from having a mission statement? If you currently have one, how have you benefited from having one?

My MS helps me refocus throughout the year. Sometimes I'll invest time in a project for a few months, and when I revisit my MS, it confirms/denies if the full fruit of that activity is aligned with where I want to head.

3.   What would you say are your top 4 values and how do they impact your decision-making?

I don't have these figured out yet, but off the top of my head: Unity (with God, my husband, my ideal readers), Dreaming Big, Faith (to believe I can actually accomplish the dream), Courage (to complete the vision, even when it's tough and lonely; to be honest & transparent even when I'm unsure if I'm "right").

4.   How do you set daily and weekly goals?

I set monthly goals, and break down the bite-sized tasks into daily or weekly tasks. But I don't set weekly goals except for a work project.

5. How would you describe the value you bring to another person right now?

I challenge people to really dig into what they believe about God, especially the parts of their theology that don't make sense to them. I try to challenge my readers and friends in convos to not rely on rote, antiquated Sunday school answers about life, purpose, God, etc., but to ponder their own ideas about who they believe God to be and what their individual purposes are in life.

6. How do you pick and choose the people in your life? Would you say it is a conscious decision?

It's absolutely a conscious decision. I choose people who have different backgrounds than me, so we can discuss differing points of view even if we aren't on the same path/life stage/ etc. I also choose people who are willing to help me grow — they discuss their line of thinking as much as the conclusive thoughts (open-minded). And then I choose people who will love and support me and allow me to do the same for them (open-hearted, loyal, forgiving).

7. What do you do to "fill your cup" and those around you?

I try to stay in a continual state of prayer with the Spirit, and then laughing a lot, meditation, yoga, reading, purposely daydreaming (5–10 min break in the middle of a work session to let my mind relax), eat well, exercise, play hard, travel.

8.   What are common fires in your life that you deal with and how do you deal with them?

This makes me think directly to emotional fires . . . I go to therapy, I pray a lot, I ask for help from my husband, deep talk with friends.

9.   What is a common habit or life habit you use that has made you successful?

Breathing techniques. It helps to de-stress quickly, to think before speaking, to know when I need to ponder something overnight before responding. It's also a great indication that I'm too wound up in work—if my breathing is stuttered, maybe I need to take a break.

10. Do you think your life would have been different by thinking of it as being the CEO? If so, how?

I already think of myself as a CEO ☺

SURVEY 2

My commentary:

This is a classic starter-in-progress. They know the CEO for Life map is important, but have not quite got the discipline in place to follow it all. This person most likely feels a lot like their life is on a roller coaster. The CEO for Life map helps compress the curve of the life roller coaster. The more you invest in the map, the shorter the ups and downs become.

1. Do you have a personal Vision and Mission Statement? Is it written down?

Be a decent person

2. How could you benefit from having a mission statement? If you currently have one, how have you benefited from having one?

Just something to keep me on track daily.

3. What would you say are your top 4 values and how do they impact your decision-making?

Be grateful; always learn; be aware.

4. How do you set daily and weekly goals?

I don't.

5. How would you describe the value you bring to another person right now?

Care and love in spite of challenges.

6. How do you pick and choose the people in your life? Would you say it is a conscious decision?

Common interests and life philosophy. Yes—1000 percent a conscious decision

7. What do you do to "fill your cup" and those around you?

Laugh, cook, give.

8. What are common fires in your life that you deal with and how do you deal with them?

Work stressors, bad manager—meditation and laughter.

9. What is a common habit or life habit you use that has made you successful?

Be organized.

10. Do you think your life would have been different by thinking of it as being the CEO? If so, how?

Better prioritization and focus.

SURVEY 3

My commentary:

This is a mature professional that knows what they should be doing and the benefits of vision, mission, values, etc. The fact is we often come to a stage in life where we feel it will not make much of a difference to start the CEO for Life map. This is farthest from the truth. Bringing the CEO mindset can happen at any time, any stage, and in any personal or professional environment. This person knows the benefits are there and is their own worst obstacle in that they have not started. Start from where you are.

1. Do you have a personal Vision and Mission Statement? Is it written down?

No.

2. How could you benefit from having a mission statement? If you currently have one, how have you benefited from having one?

Gives you a target to aim for as well as something to lean on during the hard times.

3. What would you say are your top 4 values and how do they impact your decision-making?

Positivity wins. Be kind. Always try to practice patience. Laugh a lot! If I can stay in alignment with the above mentioned, my days are happier.

4. How do you set daily and weekly goals?

Define what my success criteria is, and work backward.

5. How would you describe the value you bring to another person right now?

I try to add value to everyone I meet by being kind, positive, and empathetic.

6. How do you pick and choose the people in your life? Would you say it is a conscious decision?

It has become more of a conscious decision recently. I am seeking out higher quality and like-minded friends now.

7. What do you do to "fill your cup" and those around you?

I will work on me for you, if you work on you for me. Jim Rohn Prayer, Meditation, learning about myself, giving my time, exercise.

8. What are common fires in your life that you deal with and how do you deal with them?

Limiting beliefs. Not good enough. Imposter syndrome. Being able to identify these fires early is key. Once identified, pause, take a breath, think of something I am grateful for, and then decide on what my next right action will be.

9. What is a common habit or life habit you use that has made you successful?

The power of a positive mindset.

10. Do you think your life would have been different by thinking of it as being the CEO? If so, how?

Yes. I wish I had found this mindset as a younger man. Once I realized that I am responsible and in control of my life and stopped letting my days just happen is when I found actual happiness.

SURVEY 4

My commentary:

This response hits on almost all CEO for Life mapping cylinders. Vision, mission, and values are clear, as well as whom they surround themselves with; firefighting is understood and limiting beliefs are squashed. I would venture to say much of that comes from a spiritual foundation being strong. I touch on spiritual foundation some in the mapping process, but that must be very personal and not mandated like a map. However, I do highly recommend finding your north star spiritually. It will provide a firm foundation to work from.

1. Do you have a personal Vision and Mission Statement? Is it written down?

Yes, I do. It revolves around my calling. However, I do not have it written down.

2. How could you benefit from having a mission statement? If you currently have one, how have you benefited from having one?

Having a mission statement allows me to focus in on what should be a priority in my life as well as how to accomplish that mission.

3. What would you say are your top 4 values and how do they impact your decision-making?

1) positive outlook, 2) others come first, 3) do everything out of love, 4) keep God at the center. All of these impact my decisions by aligning values to action. I can't do something that doesn't line up with the Bible. I can't do anything that places my needs before others...

4. How do you set daily and weekly goals?

I make a list every Monday. It has a to-do list/ goal list and then action steps to meet those goals.

5. How would you describe the value you bring to another person right now?

I feel as though what I try to do is help people. I don't think I could ever assign that value. If they value it: awesome. If they do not value my help, I still will because ultimately it isn't about me!

6. How do you pick and choose the people in your life? Would you say it is a conscious decision?

I do make a conscious decision about who is in my life. I want people that will be in my life for life! They don't have to be perfect, just similar values to me.

7. What do you do to "fill your cup" and those around you?

Invest in my relationship with God. If I am right with God, He gives me strength to help others and be there for so many more than if I try to do it on my own.

8. What are common fires in your life that you deal with and how do you deal with them?

Students giving up on themselves. I remind them of their value as someone who is created for a purpose. I remind them that I love them and will be here for them as long as there is breath in my lungs.

9. What is a common habit or life habit you use that has made you successful?

Always try to push the limit on what you can do for others, not for recognition, but for the Love that we can spread. Also never treat anything as below me, if I can serve someone by helping them pick up trash or push their car then I will. I will never be "too big" for a job.

10. Do you think your life would have been different by thinking of it as being the CEO? If so, how?

Sure, I believe in some ways I am, but ultimately my CEO will always be God, I answer to Him always. If he wasn't my CEO then my choices probably would've looked a lot different in my past.

SURVEY 5

My commentary:

I want to focus only on one word in this response and that is "purpose" I deliberately stayed away from purpose as a main topic, because the ingredients of purpose can be found in vision, mission, values, and goals. So much has been written about purpose and I do not want to discount purpose. However, I do want you to know that purpose is a mix of the ingredients mentioned prior. Knowing your purpose is great, but being able to articulate it and break it down into its components is super valuable.

1. Do you have a personal Vision and Mission Statement? Is it written down?

Yes and yes.

2. How could you benefit from having a mission statement? If you currently have one, how have you benefited from having one?

It allows me to focus on my purpose. Especially during the rough patches.

3. What would you say are your top 4 values and how do they impact your decision-making?

Faith, Family, Fuel, Fun. Greatly impact my decision-making. They help me make decisions that are in alignment with my purpose.

4. How do you set daily and weekly goals?

I could do a better job at that. I'm focused on the big picture right now.

5. How would you describe the value you bring to another person right now?

I help people dig deeper.

6. How do you pick and choose the people in your life? Would you say it is a conscious decision?

I look at them as non-coincidental Divine Appointments.

7. What do you do to "fill your cup" and those around you?

Pray and pour into the lives of others.

8. What are common fires in your life that you deal with and how do you deal with them?

Fear and doubt. I have to constantly remind myself that God created me for a purpose and that my faith has to be greater than my fear.

9. What is a common habit or life habit you use that has made you successful?

Persistent and tenacious professionalism.

10. Do you think your life would have been different by thinking of it as being the CEO? If so, how?

Yes. I would [have] built my own company years ago.

SURVEY 6

My commentary:

Here is a wonderful reinforcement of the filtering process. Having a mindset and map for CEO for Life, one is able to filter the day. What is important; what can be put on hold; what doesn't deserve my energy. This response also details a morning practice or habit that sets the tone for the day. Few successful people do not have morning habits. I recently started not even looking at my phone for the first hour of the morning. I am able to focus on the other things and not feel distracted. It was hard at first, I will admit.

1. Do you have a personal Vision and Mission Statement? Is it written down?

Yes. No.

2. How could you benefit from having a mission statement? If you currently have one, how have you benefited from having one?

It keeps my family's focus on one thing. It's a filter for all of our decisions.

3. What would you say are your top 4 values and how do they impact your decision-making?

Faithfulness. Integrity. Excellence. Finishing. They guide my everyday life in work and family, and they point me to honoring Jesus regardless of the task at hand.

4. How do you set daily and weekly goals?

Yes, both. I use Michael Hyatt's full focus planner. Each week has a Big 3 and every day has 3 projects I work on related to the Big 3.

5. How would you describe the value you bring to another person right now?

I want my life to always be used for the building up of others. I call it discipleship because that's what God calls it, but basically pouring out my life in love to grow those around me for the glory of God.

6. How do you pick and choose the people in your life? Would you say it is a conscious decision?

Yes, it's absolutely conscious. I want to position myself around those who I want to become, or those in need.

7. What do you do to "fill your cup" and those around you?

For me to "fill my cup" it requires me to first know what I need, and plan it. If I don't plan it, it won't happen. For me, it's disconnecting and setting down work for a small period of time. It's healthy.

8. What are common fires in your life that you deal with and how do you deal with them?

There are fires every day, and mine typically spark out of cross-cultural miscommunication. Prayer is the only way to have a light to get through the darkness in these trials.

9. What is a common habit or life habit you use that has made you successful?

My mornings—without them, I'd be a wreck. I get up before everyone else, even the dog, to sit quietly, read, connect with God, and let my heart be still before I face the day. This habit is the healthiest rhythm in my life.

10. Do you think your life would have been different by thinking of it as being the CEO? If so, how?

Probably yes. I don't think that way, but I understand how managing my own life would help drive me toward goals.

SURVEY 7

My commentary:

My favorite take-away from this set of responses, is this person already thinks of their family as an organization. Each person in the family has a role based on their skills, their knowledge, what they are passionate about. Going back to CEO for Life as a concept, it doesn't need to be a in a boardroom; it is as easy to implement in the living room.

1. Do you have a personal Vision and Mission Statement? Is it written down?

Yes, I did strategic and business planning. Keeps us focused.

2. How could you benefit from having a mission statement? If you currently have one, how have you benefited from having one?

Keeps us focused, current, and celebrates the victories.

3. What would you say are your top 4 values and how do they impact your decision-making?

Integrity, Disciple of Christ, Consistency, Caring

4. How do you set daily and weekly goals?

iPad, yellow pad, e-mails. My husband and I hold each other accountable—Goals are only dreams with deadlines (Pat Riley)

5.   How would you describe the value you bring to another person right now?

I listen I care.

6.   How do you pick and choose the people in your life? Would you say it is a conscious decision?

Very carefully. Takes a long time. If I am being real, I probably don't trust people for a long time before I do. It's good to watch people, particularly during a tough time.

7.   What do you do to "fill your cup" and those around you?

Laughter, hugs, helping others when they need help. Watching and being a small part of their journey.

8.   What are common fires in your life that you deal with and how do you deal with them?

My daughter and son-in-law have marital challenges. We have a tenant that financially has issues in two locations. Pray, listen, try to help them find answers without being overbearing.

9.   What is a common habit or life habit you use that has made you successful?

I am an early riser. I sleep very little.

10. Do you think your life would have been different by thinking of it as being the CEO? If so, how?

My mother was a leader. She instilled this into us as an early age. She was the CEO of our family if the truth was known. Daddy was a kind bookkeeper. David is probably the CEO of our family. I am the CFO. We work together to execute them.

SURVEY 8

My commentary:

The key takeaway from this survey has to do with the unconscious and conscious shareholders in our life. It is very common to allow people in unintentionally, and then remove them intentionally. There would be less removing if the letting in had more intention.

1. Do you have a personal Vision and Mission Statement? Is it written down?

Yes.

2. How could you benefit from having a mission statement? If you currently have one, how have you benefited from having one?

Helps me stay focused and helps others understand my why.

3. What would you say are your top 4 values and how do they impact your decision-making?

Honesty, Integrity, Faith, Sincerity. If you have those, you will make the right decisions for all involved.

4. How do you set daily and weekly goals?

Yes absolutely. I set them yearly and then adjust and recheck.

5. How would you describe the value you bring to another person right now?

Support.

6. How do you pick and choose the people in your life? Would you say it is a conscious decision?

Not always conscious when they come in, it can happen organically. It's conscious when I remove them though.

7. What do you do to "fill your cup" and those around you?

Give back when I can, even in small ways, sharing clothes we don't wear, taking food to someone who is sick etc. doesn't have to cost a lot of money or take a ton of time.

8. What are common fires in your life that you deal with and how do you deal with them?

Managing people with different backgrounds and personalities. Take a step back prior to reacting and keeping in mind you don't know what they are going through.

9. What is a common habit or life habit you use that has made you successful?

Keeping close to God weekly. Always think of other before myself.

10. Do you think your life would have been different by thinking of it as being the CEO? If so, how?

I do think of it that way. I have been 100 percent commission my entire career.

SURVEY 9

My commentary:

Quote from this survey: ". . . had my parents and people in my life told me I was the CEO of my life . . . that would have made a big difference. We have told our son (14 years old) he is the CEO of his life since he was 4 and he BELIEVES it and acts like it (most of the time)." I promise; I am not wasting your time. This mapping and thinking as a CEO will change your life. It changed mine, and I know it can change yours.

1. Do you have a personal Vision and Mission Statement? Is it written down?

Yes. It is written down. I reflect on it daily.

2. How could you benefit from having a mission statement? If you currently have one, how have you benefited from having one?

There are many days life gets busy and hectic but always reflecting on my mission statement helps get me back on track. It helps me to eliminate the "outside noise and interference" and get back to my MAIN objective.

3. What would you say are your top 4 values and how do they impact your decision-making?

INTEGRITY. Know and do what is right. SERVANT LEADERSHIP. Serve the common good in all aspects of my life. RESPECT. Treating others the way you want to be treated. RESPONSIBILITY. Embrace opportunities to contribute.

4. How do you set daily and weekly goals?

Sunday evening, I take one hour to plan my day and week ahead. I also set three goals every week that are directly related to my current workload.

5. How would you describe the value you bring to another person right now?

I would describe the value I bring to others by listing the words that describe the value I bring to another person. Dependability. Reliability. Loyalty. Commitment. Open-mindedness. Consistency. Honesty. Efficiency.

6. How do you pick and choose the people in your life? Would you say it is a conscious decision?

I am VERY intentional. You get what you inspect not what you expect. I'm a personality that makes everyone feel accepted and loved by me and even feel like they're my best friend BUT I am purposefully making others feel that way while my truth is there are only a FEW people in my "true circle" of friends.

7. What do you do to "fill your cup" and those around you?

I take a break and grab a Starbucks. I get out for dinner with a friend. I like to exercise or take a walk by myself.

8. What are common fires in your life that you deal with and how do you deal with them?

Common fires come from HR, PR, media, politics and business. There are too many fires to mention specifically but it's always the same approach. 1. Stop and make sure I know all of the details to make an informed decision. 2. Process the information and see who is and should be a part of putting the fire out. 3. Make a 3-step (or less) plan to resolve. 4. REALIZE and KNOW it's simply LIFE. Deal with it, manage it, and resolve it.

9. What is a common habit or life habit you use that has made you successful?

1. I never give up. 2. I say YES. 3. I have always connected people. 4. My energy and drive is UNMATCHED. 5. My confidence is pure and real and is part of my makeup and being.

10. Do you think your life would have been different by thinking of it as being the CEO? If so, how?

Of course. When you think like a CEO, you take on and assume all responsibility for your life (your life being your company). Naturally, the title comes with a level of ownership, humility, integrity, and responsibility. The title alone can cause one to MOVE FORWARD, THINK AT A HIGHER LEVEL, and be BETTER. Yes, had my parents and people in my life told me I was the CEO of my life . . . that would have made a big difference. We have told our son (14 years old) he is the CEO of his life since he was 4 and he BELIEVES it and acts like it (most of the time).

SURVEY 10

My commentary:

This response is particularly interesting from the "whom you surround yourself with" perspective. This respondent had a specific formula for what they look for in those they allow in their sphere or close to them. As I mentioned in the book, you are an average of those with whom you surround yourself. I highly recommend auditing who are you giving your time to and who are you allowing to pour into you. If I could just convince you to make some CEO changes in your life in this area, you would see a major impact and push forward to your dreams.

1. Do you have a personal Vision and Mission Statement? Is it written down?

Help people be the happiest, healthiest, strongest, & most fulfilled version of themselves. Reach the person that needs us most at the moment they need us with the message they need. Don't know who they are, where they are or what they need but every day we push out good thoughts in hopes of reaching them at the moment they need it most.

2. How could you benefit from having a mission statement? If you currently have one, how have you benefited from having one?

North Star guiding the journey in life.

3. What would you say are your top 4 values and how do they impact your decision-making?

Love Health Adventure Freedom. Use them daily to guide all decisions.

4. How do you set daily and weekly goals?

What do I want Why do I want it How will I achieve it.

5. How would you describe the value you bring to another person right now?

Life changing results.

6. How do you pick and choose the people in your life? Would you say it is a conscious decision?

Yes—33 percent a few steps ahead on the journey. 33 percent at the same moment of the journey, 33 percent a few steps behind. Learn it—Live it—give it

7. What do you do to "fill your cup" and those around you?

Be present & love them with all my might.

8. What are common fires in your life that you deal with and how do you deal with them?

As a team! My wife and I always have each other's back and work through everything together.

9.   What is a common habit or life habit you use that has made you successful?

Ability to build and maintain positive habits. Growth mindset.

10. Do you think your life would have been different by thinking of it as being the CEO? If so, how?

No.

SURVEY 11

My commentary:

I do not dive too far into the idea of foundations in this book. This book is more meant to be actionable. What I love about this response and what I would like to highlight is that every CEO for Life needs a foundation to work from. Morals and values come from somewhere. Finding your foundation in decision-making forms your values and morals.

1.   Do you have a personal Vision and Mission Statement? Is it written down?

Love God. Love Others.

2.   How could you benefit from having a mission statement? If you currently have one, how have you benefited from having one?

A mission statement for life helps you define your purpose. How many people do you know could grab a sheet of paper, write at the top of it "My purpose in life is…" and be able to complete the sentence? It took me years to complete that sentence, and that was with several wise men helping define my gifts and strengths.

3.   What would you say are your top 4 values and how do they impact your decision-making?

God, Family, Country, Others. They help prioritize my focus on other.

4. How do you set daily and weekly goals?

I set goals every week to get my workload done, but I have learned to not "stack the load" and therefore leave no room for my wife and children. My relationship with my wife is the cornerstone for my family. My relationship with my children is directly tied to my quality time with my wife. My ability to lead well at work is tied to the previous two things. How we treat others is a direct reflection on how healthy our home life is. So, that being said, my weekly goal is a balance of time…knowing when to jump in early, and knowing when to shut things down.

5. How would you describe the value you bring to another person right now?

As leaders, we bring value to others every moment of every day. If we do not, we won't be leaders very long. It is a stewardship of relationships.

6. How do you pick and choose the people in your life? Would you say it is a conscious decision?

Very conscious. Time is limited, and we need to be stewards of that time. I choose to be around others that bring encouragement and knowledge. I choose to be around people that have their own lives in order, with life goals and purpose known. When I spend time with like-minded leaders, I can better serve others and build others up. It's an equipping process that prepares.

7. What do you do to "fill your cup" and those around you?

I serve others. There is nothing better for your focus on things that matter than to stop and serve. By giving time and resources you "fill your cup." The other area is solitude. This is important for anyone, but it can be taken too far. Build times of solitude into your schedule…no people…no phone, and you will see what I mean. Start with 30 minutes a week.

8. What are common fires in your life that you deal with and how do you deal with them?

Conflict. The common thread in any business or ministry. If handled well you will strengthen your team. Conflict can be a "good thing." We deal with conflict within our team quickly . . . "Hey Bob, can we talk?" is all that needs to be said to start diffusing and start building.

9. What is a common habit or life habit you use that has made you successful?

Prayer.

10. Do you think your life would have been different by thinking of it as being the CEO? If so, how?

I'm not sure what is being asked here.

About the Author

Robert Lee Barber credits his work ethic to being raised by a single mom. Robert is a degreed Electrical Engineer who found a passion for people and joined the Human Resources profession. He helped a Fortune 150 company expand from two states to twenty-six states and over three thousand employees before taking the leap into entrepreneurship.

In 2006, he left his Senior HR position to test his mettle in real estate. With the 2006 and 2007 recession, Robert was looking at the road to broke-town until he and his business partner created a real estate auction company conducting more than 800 real estate auctions and then consulted for money management firms. With two companies under his belt, this led to a wonderful partnership in a retail start-up real estate firm in 2012. He and his partners grew that company to $917 million in sales in 2018.

In 2019, Robert exited the firm to pursue his passion for people once again, moving from Florida to Chattanooga, Tennessee (Gig City). Feeling he had accumulated enough tools, skills, and battle scars in his bag of tricks, he launched *Return On Your Investment Academy*, with a focus on organizational and individual professional performance consulting.

Robert has been married for twenty-four years and has two daughters.